P9-DDN-672

How to Be a *People Magnet*

How to Be a *People Magnet*

Finding Friends—and Lovers—and Keeping Them for Life

LEIL LOWNDES

CB
CONTEMPORARY BOOKS

21140067

Library of Congress Cataloging-in-Publication Data

Lowndes, Leil.
    How to be a people magnet : finding friends—and lovers—and
keeping them for life / Leil Lowndes.
       p.   cm.
    ISBN 0-8092-2434-8
     1. Interpersonal relations.   2. Interpersonal communication.
3. Friendship.   4. Love.   I. Title.
HM1106.L68   2000
302—dc21   00-34550
                                                 CIP

Cover design by Scott Rattray
Interior design by Mary Lockwood

Published by Contemporary Books
A division of NTC/Contemporary Publishing Group, Inc.
4255 West Touhy Avenue, Lincolnwood (Chicago), Illinois 60712-1975 U.S.A.
Copyright © 2001 by Leil Lowndes
All rights reserved. No part of this book may be reproduced, stored in a
retrieval system, or transmitted in any form or by any means, electronic,
mechanical, photocopying, recording, or otherwise, without the prior written
permission of NTC/Contemporary Publishing Group, Inc.
Printed in the United States of America
International Standard Book Number: 0-8092-2434-8
01 02 03 04 05 06 MV 18 17 16 15 14 13 12 11 10 9 8 7 6 5 4 3 2 1

Dedicated to my dearest friends Giorgio and Phil
who taught me the meaning of the words
love and friendship.

♡ Contents

How to Be a *People Magnet*

Part One

On the Road to Being a People Magnet

I   Friends, Lovers, and Knights

"I get by with a little help from my friends."

—JOHN LENNON

It's *not* just a song. We all need a little help from our friends. If not now, tomorrow. Or the day after. Or the year after. Some people never realize it until it's too late. They invest in stocks, bonds, or real estate thinking money is going to give them the security and happiness they seek. Sadly, they neglect the most important investment of their lives—time spent finding, making, and nurturing true friendships and true lasting love relationships.

Sometimes we are a nation of blockheads so blinded by sex, that we don't see the true love for the birds and the bees. (Not that there's anything wrong with the birds and the bees—we're going to talk about those captivating little critters. But with no myths, no false magic.) We're going to *get real* about love and sex. Because all too often the lovebird sings sweet lies, and the bee stings too hard. We're also going to talk about friendship because, as we mature, same-sex and other-sex nonsexual friends take on an increasingly important role in our lives.[1]

Here are some of the types of relationships we're going to explore in *How to Be a People Magnet*.

Platonic Friendships

There's No Such Thing! (Or Is There?)

Many people, especially men, say there's no such thing as a *platonic* (as in *no sex*) friendship between a man and a woman—unless the two just plain don't find each other sexually attractive.

The issue is further complicated by differing definitions of a platonic relationship. I asked one of my girlfriends to define a platonic relationship and her quick answer, devoid of emotion, was "It is a friendship with an esteemed and appreciated individual of the male gender with whom sexual intercourse is neither advantageous nor desired."

I then asked a male friend to define it. His answer, filled with angst, was "A platonic relationship is a transparent and sadistic ruse by which attractive and otherwise eligible females smash a male acquaintance who shows romantic interest to smithereens by announcing to said acquaintance, 'I just want to be friends.'" He paused, put his head in his hands, and added sadly, "Thereby ripping out the poor schnook's heart and shredding it to pieces." He admitted that he had once been emotionally clobbered by a woman with that cruel club called "I just want to be friends."

Excuse me, if I I may interject my opinion here (after all, I *am* the author of this book), I definitely feel men and women can have a platonic relationship. I should know, I have a great one. In fact he's more than a friend, he's my roommate! (New York City apartment prices make strange *non*-bedfellows.) Phil's candor about his various triumphs and tribulations with the weaker (ha!) sex will flesh out and corroborate many of the studies upon which this book is based.

And, of Course, Love

The Magic That Makes the World Go 'Round.

Ah, yes, love. Love between a man and a woman is so mysterious, so miraculous, so marvelous it defies simple definition. It is the most deranged, delusive, and yet strangely most desired state of all. This is the one we say we have no control over. We don't speak of *falling in friendship* or *falling into a network* against our will. Yet we talk of falling in love, as if we tumbled into the boat against our will.

Once we've fallen into the love boat, most of us forget to inspect the hull to see if it's full of holes. We don't even look at the charts to see where the relationship is going to take us! It's a beautiful sunny day so we just smile, hoist the sails, and let the winds take us out to sea.

He called? He sent flowers? He told you he loves you? It's like a huge wave lifting you to the crest and you feel like you're on top of the world. You laugh, you talk, you sing, you dance, you make love and your universe is spinning.

She said she's not ready for a relationship? She wants to be *just friends*? You suspect she's seeing someone else? The wave crashes, you're sucked under, and you think you're drowning.

Now the early sunshine turns to a black sky, an ominous foreshadowing of a tempestuous storm. Blinded by the wind and the waves, you're unable to steer the relationship and keep your balance in the rocky love boat. It becomes a nightmare from which you can't awake!

We're going to talk a lot about love—how to get it, how to give it, how to keep it. You'll also get some navigation lessons on how to circumvent the storms.

Men's Friendships

"I Love Ya, Man!"

In the nineteenth century, men formed deep bonds with each other, confided the most intimate details of their lives, wrote letters of love to each other, and even slept in the same bed. But gay? No way! These friendships were not only accepted, they were respected by both men and women.[2] Today men run like dogs with cans tied to their tails when the subject of deep feelings for each other comes up.

In fact, some men even have trouble coughing up the words, "my friend." Manny, an old college chum, is like that. Over the years I've heard him talk about John, his closest friend. He'll say,

"John, yeah, he's my main man," or my "pardner." Or maybe, "my amigo," "my compadre."

If he does say the "f-word" ("Friend") he toughens it up with a string of virile adjectives. When I started writing this book, I asked him, "Manny, how many men friends do you have?" Like it was a new word in his vocabulary, he scratched his head and responded, "Friends? You mean buddies, honest-to-goodness, ignore-their-buck-naked-wife *friends*?"

"Well, yeah, Manny, I guess you could say that. Isn't there some guy you like whose relationship isn't based 100 percent on chasing babes, booze, or baseball? Some guy who really knows you and understands you?"

He shrugged and said, "Understands me? Most men don't need to be completely understood." I could sense from his smug smile he felt good about expressing that tidbit of ideology.

But it quickly disappeared when I asked, "OK, who can you share your feelings with?"

Manny rubbed his neck and said, "Oh come on, Leil. You're not going to give me any of that old Robert Bly stuff, are you? I think I know what you're getting at. But I'm not one of those cream puffs who starts beating drums and dancing naked back in the woods to get in touch with my infantile self.

"Women wanting us to express our feelings (his nose scrunched at the word) presumes we have feelings. And, sure, we've got one or two. But they remain submerged and, if we air them, it violates their validity." Then, pointing one finger in the air as though making a profound philosophical statement, Manny pronounced, "The strength of the genie, comes from being in a bottle.

"And," he added, "You can put that in your pipe and smoke it!"

I decided not to pursue it further—for the moment.

Women's Friendships

"Oh, Why Can't a Man Be More like a Woman?"

At least that's how most women feel about friendship. We're the self-proclaimed experts on friendship. But are we really?

How do you define being an expert on friendship? If you define it as having more friends, it's women.[3] If you define it as being more sensitive to each other's unspoken needs, it's women.[4] If you define it as genuinely liking their female friends better than anyone in the world, it's women. (One study showed many women like their best friends better than their husbands!)[5] If you define it as talking about their friendships and admitting them more openly than the *less gentle sex*, it's women.[6] If you ask who is able to receive more comfort from their same-sex friends in later life, it's women.[7] If you define it as knowing the intimate details of their friends' lives, it's women. (Seat any two women together on a long train trip and, by the time they reach their destination, they could write a novel about each other. Seat typical males together at adjoining desks, and two years later most don't know each other's wives' names—or if they even have wives!)

If you define it as knowing that having friends helps you live longer; improves your immune system; slows the aging process; and reduces the incidences of colds, flu, high blood pressure, and heart disease, it's women.[8] All pretty strong evidence that women are better at friendship. But, experts? We'll see.

Networking Friends

So Who Are These Knights?

Most people, if they decide to take a major vacation say, "It was lucky we have our friend, Tom, the Travel Agent." If they get sued, "It's lucky we have our friend, Laura, the Lawyer." If their dog Goofy gets sick, "It's lucky we have our friend, Vinnie, the Vet." And so on through every situation that sooner or later hits them in the face. And even though, if you were a betting man or woman, you would place bets that a particular something would never happen, that particular something *always* happens—and *always* catches you by surprise.

Was it just luck that Tom, Laura, and Vinnie were friends when you decided to go globe-trotting, when you got sued for leaving a banana peel on your sidewalk, or when Goofy got green around the gills?

Not if you're smart. Everyone needs Toms, Lauras, and Vinnies in their life, and a lot of other friends with a vast selection of skills upon whom they can call in times of need. I call these folks, both men and women, *knights*.

For the analogy, I went back—way back—to when I was all curled up in my flannel jammies, hugging my teddy bear about to drift off to sleep. Mamma is reading my favorite story to me. . . .

There is a sword stuck in a stone, and whoever could pull it out would become king. Nobody succeeded until a freckle-faced kid named Arthur comes along and slides it out like a knife out of butter. He then becomes king, King Arthur, and marries a fair maiden named Guinevere. The part I liked best was right after the wedding when Merlin the magician rises, toasts King Arthur and his new Queen Guinevere, clears his throat, and speaks in solemn tones.

"Today is the first day of the *Knights of the Round Table*; you all have your allotted chairs. No seat is more important than any other. But when one knight dies, another will take his place, with the name on the seat changing by itself. With that," he said, "I leave you now to the wise counsel of your King. Good-bye and God bless you all."

When Merlin had taken his leave, King Arthur rose and called for silence. Often the last words I'd hear before entering dreamland, was King Arthur asking each knight, "Are you loyal to your King, and to each other?" Sometimes I tried to stay awake to hear each of the 150 knights swearing their sacred oath in sequence, "One for all, and all for one." But I usually fell asleep by the time I got to the fourth or fifth knight.

I didn't mind though because my knights came back for an encore in my dreams. They would slay fire-breathing dragons snorting gusts of purple smoke and orange flames and rescue damsels in distress. These visions made me feel safe all day long. I truly believed that King Arthur and the Knights of the Round Table were real and would magically appear to rescue me if ever I should need them.

But just as King Arthur had to do without Merlin one day, I grew up and had to do without believing that King Arthur and

his knights were real. So now I've replaced the valiant mythological Knights of the Round Table with real ones. I have *knights*,
both female and male, who will slay any dragon of a problem for
me and rescue me when I am in distress. And, of course, I will slay
any of their dragons within my realm of possibility. One for all,
and all for one. In modern day parlance, it's called a *network*, and
we all need a good one.

How do I know that? Because something really really bad
happened to me one summer—something I'll tell you about
later—and if I'd had my druthers it never would have happened.
But it changed my life forever and made me realize that love and
friendship—giving it and getting it—is the most important thing
in life.

So if you are ready to start filling your life with friendship,
love, and a terrific support system, let's go! Have your pen filled
with ink so you can sign off on some of the clauses in this personal contract between you and yourself, and mark the ones you'll
have to come back to. You're making a plan that will enrich the
rest of your life. And maybe, some day, it will even save it, like it
did mine.

By the way, while carefully constructing this plan, don't forget to enjoy the journey. As he also wrote before he was gunned
down in the driveway of the Dakota,

*"Life is what happens while you're busy making
other plans."*
—John Lennon

2 What's Ahead in *How to Be a People Magnet*

I bet you know some folks who are human magnets. It's not that they're overly good-looking, rich, or bright. But they walk into a room of strangers, and people smile. They walk into a singles' bar, people stare. They walk into a negotiation, and the suits on the other side of the table instinctively smell, "They are big time."

If they're single, everyone wants to be their date. If married, passionate partners are grateful to be their mate. If they're in need, faithful friends would charge over the hill, run through fire, or walk on broken glass for them.

But wait a minute! They don't have anything you haven't got—maybe less. So what's the secret?

That's what *How to Be a People Magnet* is all about.

How We're Going to Find the Answer

From the time we are little tykes rattling the rails of our cribs to get attention, until the time we catch a cloud to carry us to the great beyond, we want people to like us. Kids call it *popularity* whereas adults prefer *charisma*, or *leadership ability*. But even if the generations can't agree on a word for *it*, they know what it is. And everybody wants *it*.

Usually people classify this coveted talent in three parts. When talking about business, they say "communications skills." When referring to being comfortable with strangers and making friends, it's "social skills." And when love is in the air, the ability to win hearts is all important. Then they say someone has "sex appeal."

Having researched exhaustively, lectured extensively, and written books on all three subjects, I want to let you in on a little secret. *It's all the same thing!* Quite simply, it's that quintessential quality that makes people like you and want to be part of your world today, tomorrow, or forever. And that's what we're going to learn in *How to Be a People Magnet*. Each section gives you another way to enrich your life through finding loyal friends and true love.

Part Two, "Making Strangers Like You, Instantly!," gives you confidence booster shots and party tactics. Then it teaches you some lovely little tricks to spread sunshine and make strangers smile, wherever you go.

Part Three, "Friends and Lovers," is about finding, then binding, friendships and romantic love. It shows you how to find a wide variety of people to enhance your life and then walk the talk that most people only talk. If, as Shakespeare said, "All the world's a stage, and all the men and women merely players," this section helps you choose the players you want in your life, then gives you ways to win them—and qualities to *keep* them.

Part Four, "Cupid's Secrets," reveals some surprising truths that the cunning little cherub tried to hide from us, but recent research has excavated. We've turned these nuggets into sexy schemes you can use to lure lovers—and keep them!

Part Five, "Networking," helps you build a solid support system of people with a vast array of skills. Like King Arthur and his Knights of the Round Table, you will emerge with an army which may someday save your life, as it did mine.

The Fatal FUD Factor
(Fear, Uncertainty, and Doubt)

Throughout the book we work on eliminating the number one people repellant: Fear, Uncertainty, and Doubt—that fatal FUD factor.

Norman Vincent Peale spent twenty-five years trying to stamp out the FUD Factor. He knew the world was already too full of worrywarts and wet blankets who believe the only thing the world will ever give them on a silver platter is tarnish. Hundreds of motivational speakers and feel-good gurus since Norman have tried to inject our brains and veins with positive-thinking juice to get rid of it. But it's easier said than done. You don't make it go away by standing on a chair, beating your chest, and shouting, "I'm the best! Everybody loves me!"

Even Dale Carnegie tried to teach us how to win friends and influence people. He did a really good job, but he neglected two crucial factors. When it comes to finding friends and lovers, one size does *not* fit all. Those folks who can pick and choose their friends and lovers found *that* fallacy years ago.

Another fumble that success coaches make is they give us *their* opinion of what works—or what's worked for *them*—not what's been proved in controlled studies conducted by responsible researchers around the world. *How to Be a People Magnet* is different from any other book on relationships in that specific sociological, anthropological, or psychological studies support everything I say.

Most motivators make a third big mistake. They tell us what to do—and then they don't even wait to see if we agree. They preach from the podium, then step down to great applause, but little commitment from the audience to comply. Or they write a book and, when readers finish the last page, they close the book—and all too often, their commitment to comply.

How to Be a People Magnet isn't going to let you get away with that! You are going to be asked to read this book with a pen in your hand to sign clauses and a promise in your heart to comply.

3 ♡ Why This Book Is *Guaranteed* to Work!

Many books offer relationship advice, but what sets this book apart is that you'll learn specific skills that will enhance your ability to be a people magnet. Theories make for interesting reading, but growth comes from putting the theories into practice.

This Is Not a Book—It's a Contract

The first reason that *How to Be a People Magnet* is guaranteed to work is, it's a contract—a very personal contract between you and the person you are most responsible to in life—yourself.

The definition of a contract according to our dearly departed, but oft-quoted, Noah Webster is "a binding agreement usually between two or more persons or parties." Since we all have "two or more persons" residing within ourselves, we'll take liberties with *two*.

Women, looking in the mirror, are continually having conversations like this one with themselves:

You #1: Shall I wear these old jeans today?
You #2: Nah, they make you look like a busted sofa!

You #1: They're not *that* bad, and tight jeans are sexy.
You #2: What, are you kidding? You look like you were poured into them and forgot to say "when."

Or, you're a single man asking yourself,

You #1: Should I ask her out?
You #2: Of course, not, stupid. She'll say "no."
You #1: Yeah, but if I don't ask her, I'll never know. What if she says "yes?"
You #2: You? Lamebrain! Why would a gorgeous woman like her want to go out with an ugly-ass blot-on-the-landscape like you?"

And so the two factions within you slug it out. But not to worry, soon you'll know how to write a contract between the internal warring parties so your best side always wins.

How to Be a People Magnet has many clauses. Don't worry if you can't promise to comply with every single one. Neither can I—yet (but I'm working at it). All I ask is that you consider each clause carefully. Then, if—and only if—you agree to make the suggestion a part of your life, put your signature on the dotted line. The ones that are primarily for men are marked ♂. The clauses marked ♀ are mainly for women. The rest, marked ♂ and ♀, are for both men and women alike.

Sociological Studies Support the Contract

The second reason *How to Be a People Magnet* is guaranteed to work is that almost all the clauses are backed by nonbiased sociological studies. If you should read a clause and the information I provide is not sufficient to convince you to sign the clause, then I beseech you to check the referenced numbers in the Endnotes. There you will find the proof in the original studies.

Be forewarned that most of the studies are written in a strange dialect which I call *academeeze*. This curious scholarly style gets a "10" for its precision, but only a "2" for its clarity for the layman.

Here's a sample. What do you think the following sentence means? You've got thirty seconds: "When the level of analysis of a construct is open to debate, Klein, et al. suggest that fairness and research rigor will be enhanced by measurement strategies that allow for empirical testing of appropriate levels of analysis."

Huh? You're a much better reader than I if you understood they were just saying, "When you're not sure of the results, it's better to test it in a way that's easier to measure."

In any case, I plowed sluggishly but smilingly through studies that tell us some crucial can't-live-without information, like why watching old television shows such as "Beverly Hills 90210" or "Melrose Place" can be dangerous to your health (whereas watching "Roseanne" or "Designing Women" isn't!), or why men love helping women with some problems but not others—and where they draw the line.

I took the often surprising results of these studies and put them into plain English. Sometimes, I fear, it's in too plain English. I hope you and the serious researchers will forgive the linguistic liberties I've taken with their very significant works.

Listen to the Testimonials

The third reason that *How to Be a People Magnet* is guaranteed to work is: it contains confidential testimony from thousands of individuals in my relationships seminars.

For eight years, I have been conducting communications-skills and relationship seminars all over the English-speaking world, and I have perhaps learned as much from my students as they have from me—especially when it comes to the confusion men and women have about each other. The two sexes continue to baffle each other in the boardroom, the bedroom, and beyond. Yet they are hesitant to ask, "Why do you . . . ?" and "How do you really feel about . . . ?"

In both my corporate and public seminars, they can ask questions anonymously and without embarrassment by writing them on a card signing only "M" for male or "F" for female. I then put the questions to the group, and the women answer the men's questions, then vice versa. Revealing only the asker's gender has a unifying effect on the opposite sex, and they sally forth with often surprising but always sincere answers.

With these three guarantees in your pocket, fill your pen with ink so you can start signing off on the clauses that will make you into a human magnet attracting people who want to befriend you, love you, or support you.

PART TWO

MAKING STRANGERS
LIKE YOU, INSTANTLY!

4 Hi! How Do You Like Me So Far?

Think back to your college or high school days. Remember the Big Man on Campus, the Prom Queen, the Cheerleaders—the real *cool* kids. In most schools, these were the kids everyone envied. These were the kids everybody dressed like and tried to walk and talk like, and the ones they wanted to be seen strolling to class with. If you were like most teenagers, you probably wanted to date them or be their buddy. You wanted them to like you, and you hoped some of their stardust would rub off on you.

But, deep down, did you really like them? I mean *really* like them? Here's a test. Let's say you are paddling a canoe on a big lake, and suddenly you spot two men who can't swim on a quickly sinking raft. They're both howling, "Help me! Help me!" As you row frantically toward the raft, you see that one of them is Brad, the Big Man on Campus. The other is . . . oh no. It can't be! It's Dexter! He's your dorky, doggedly-devoted, forever-faithful follower from the old neighborhood where you both grew up. Your canoe is tiny, and you only have room to row one of them to safety.

Now, one hand on your heart, the other on the Bible. Who would you choose? Dexter? Of course you would. How do I know? Because, surprising new studies show that *being liked* and being *popular* in the sense that we knew in school is *not* the same thing. And when the chips are down, we help people we really like first.

But Is Being Popular *Really* Being Liked?

It's a strange phenomenon, yet it happens all over the world. As soon as two or more kids get together, they form a pecking order, just like chickens on a farm. Ask any kid, from the first grade on up, "Who are the popular kids? And who are the unpopular kids?" The little tyke will tell you immediately.[9]

Until recently, everyone thought being popular in school was, by definition, *being liked by lots of people*. But when researchers started asking school kids confidentially, "Who is popular?" and "Whom do you like?" They got a big shock. Many students did not merely dislike the popular kids, they *resented* them as well. They wanted to be in their *clique* only to increase their own status. Eleven percent of the students admitted to downright despising the kids *everyone else* considered so cool.[10]

Upon further questioning, researchers discovered that many of these *cool* kids were indeed mean.[11] They created a false sense of exclusivity by never hanging out with their less popular schoolmates. Often it was to cover their own insecurities.

What's Your Optimism Quotient (OQ)?

To find out precisely what qualities make people like us, the American Sociological Association conducted a vast study.[12] The results? At the top of the list was having a positive optimistic personality and confidence in yourself.

I'm sure you've seen the TV interviews with the athletes just before the tennis match, the football game, the wrestling match. The reporter asks the player, "Do you think you're going to win?" She replies, "Definitely." In another interview, he asks her opponent the same question and her answer is the same, "Absolutely."

Or a reporter asks a boxer, "Are you going to win?" He replies, "I'm-a gonna kill da mudder fudder." Then he asks the contender the same question. He answers, "Ha! I ain't gonna swap leather for more den fifteen seconds wit dat powder puff before he kisses da canvas."

Whenever I heard these interviews I thought, "What vulgar, crude arrogance. One of them must know he's kidding himself. Both sides can't be cocksure of success."

I'm older and wiser now, and I realize that to be successful you must be genuinely confident. You can't just put on the face of confidence for the competition—or for the meeting or the party or the date. You have to feel confidence pulsing through your veins. Your heart has to be the drum which beats out the rhythm of confidence. Every word that comes out of your mouth has to be the lyrics of confidence.

Olympic athletes don't just "get it up for the game." They practice getting into what some call *the zone* so that it's all there for the competition. Leading up to that is years of training their bodies to move instinctively, without losing precious seconds in stopping to figure out what to do next.

Likewise, you must train your body to react instinctively for success, without thinking about it. Your game isn't throwing a javelin or hurling a discus. It's waking up each day like the little engine who said, "I think I can."

Perhaps you remember the kid's story of the little engine that had to climb a big mountain. It was huffing and puffing and having horrendous difficulty. But with each huff and puff, the little train expressed, "I think I can. I think I can. I think I can." And the little engine did.

In fact, because of the little engine, I met a friend in college who remains a buddy until this day. I was at a fraternity house party and, owing to a severe case of shyness, was trying to meld into the wallpaper. Since nobody was talking to me, I ambled over to the fireplace and feigned interest in a toy wooden train engine on the mantle.

A few moments later, above my head behind me, I heard a Texas drawl, "Excuse me ma'am, but I just couldn't help but admire you while you're admiring my choo choo train there." I whirled around to find myself facing a huge chest. I slowly followed it up with my eyes until I reached the face of a tall, grinning Texan. Sensing my shyness, he proceeded to tell me a story, the story of how his father had given the engine to him when he was a kid as a symbol of I-can-do-anything thinking.

He made conversing easy and we spent the rest of the party talking ("makin' chin music," he called it). Soon we got around to the subject of what we wanted to do after college. He told me that when his dad passed away without having taken out any insurance, the family was left with nothing but the house they lived in. That inspired him to enter the field of selling life insurance.

Two things stuck in my mind about that conversation. First, Dale told me a true story—the story of what inspired him to enter the field. He didn't just wind up selling life insurance because that was the best way to make a buck. He created a true and inspiring story. (Keep that in mind because we'll get back to it later when we talk about marketing yourself the way celebrity makers market stars.)

The second characteristic I remember is the calm assurance he exuded from the top of his ten gallon hat to the tip of his pointy kill-a-cockroach-in-the-corner boots. He didn't say, "I want to sell life insurance." He didn't say, "I'll *try* to be the best life insurance man in Texas." Dale said, "I *will* be the best life insurance salesman in Texas." And today he is.

It's no wonder. People enjoy buying from him because he never lets his own problems get others down. He has a beautiful office building just on the outskirts of Dallas. During a big storm there several years ago, his roof blew off, the trees came crashing down, the office floors were badly flooded, and most of the furniture and paper records were destroyed. His phones were obviously out of order so that night I called him at home and asked if his office survived the storm.

He said, "Honey, I bet you been walkin' a hole in the carpet over this. It was blowin' so hard you could spit in your own eye. But don't you worry, everybody's fine. Though the office got plucked cleaner than a Thanksgiving turkey, we'll be back in business better 'n ever within the week."

And so he was. Even when he was talking about a torrential rainstorm, Dale was able to spread a bit of sunshine on his listeners.

5 How to Spread Sunshine ... Wherever You Go

Dale carried a pocketful of sunshine with him which made people glow wherever he went. Not only did he always look on the bright side of things, he looked at *everything* from the other person's perspective, thus winning their hearts. I think that was one of his most winning ways.

One rainy morning several years ago when I was giving a speech in Dallas, Dale and I met at a coffee shop for a very early breakfast and then a tour of his new offices. We were the only customers in the coffee shop. He placed his order by saying to the waitress, "Ma'am, I bet you hate the smell of ham and eggs this early, but . . ."

"No problem!" the waitress said, grinning from ear to ear. Dale was looking at his order from her standpoint.

Paying the tab, he said to the cashier, "How do you like that? I'm your first customer of the day, and you're stuck trying to make change from a fifty dollar bill. I sure hope it doesn't clean you out."

"No problem," said the cashier, smiling broadly and forking over the thirty-five dollars of change.

♡ More Magnetic Attraction!

Before People Magnets speak, they ask themselves,
"What is my listener thinking and feeling right now?"
Then, whenever appropriate, they speak from their
listener's perspective. For People Magnets (PMs), scowls
turn to smiles, dullness turns to delight, and *no* turns
to *yes!*

On the way to his new building, we stopped at a gas station. "Buddy, it's a durn shame you have to come out in this rain just to fill up some dude's gas tank."

"No problem, sir." Smiles.

As we entered Dale's lobby, the doorman held the door for us. Dale's greeting? "I sure am sorry. They're gonna be some sloppy galoshes messin' up your floor today." Under his big rain hat I could see the doorman's enormous no problem smile.

The phone was ringing as Dale unlocked his offices. The secretary wasn't in yet so he grabbed it. All I heard was, "I'm so sorry ma'am, you just wasted your quarter. You're going to have to look up that number again 'cause no one named Betty Ann works here." Even a wrong number got Dale's looking-at-it-from-his-listener's-perspective treatment. As he hung up, I imagined the caller smiling even though she'd just wasted her time and money on a wrong number.

I've dubbed Dale's knack of putting everything in his listener's perspective "In-Your-Shoes" communicating. Recently, I've started using it with everyone I can. The results are phenomenal! Smiles break out all over. Try it. You can use it in practically all conversations. You'll find it works especially well with strangers.

For example, suppose you are on vacation, and you are hopelessly lost. You have no idea where your hotel is. Thank heavens, you spot a policeman and you can ask directions.

Instead of saying, "Hey, where is the Midtown Hotel?" or even "Excuse me, could you tell me where the Midtown Hotel is?", you venture an "In-Your-Shoes" way of asking:

"I know it's not your job but could you direct me to the Midtown Hotel?"

"I bet you're really tired of people asking, but could you direct me to . . ."

"I bet you're thinking, 'Oh oh, here comes another lost tourist.' And you're right. But could you . . ."

"I know you're here on a much more important assignment to protect life and limb, but could you tell me where . . ."

Not only will you get a smile, you'll get extra good directions.

Here is the first clause in *How to Be a People Magnet*. Because it is for both men and women, I've marked it with both ♂ and ♀. If you are going to make a sincere effort to speak from your listener's perspective, then go ahead and sign on the dotted line. That is your commitment to yourself.

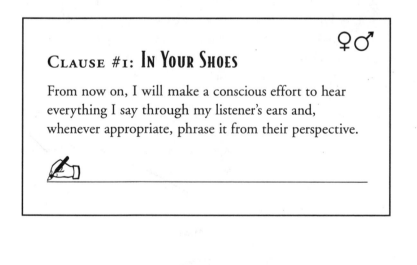

CLAUSE #1: IN YOUR SHOES   ♀♂

From now on, I will make a conscious effort to hear everything I say through my listener's ears and, whenever appropriate, phrase it from their perspective.

6 Making Everyone Feel Special

One time I complimented Dale on how he made sincere contact, no matter how brief, with everyone. His answer? "Well, why not? Why not make every moment and every person in your life count? It gives them joy and it gives you joy. It's a win-win situation."

Throughout the day, we exchange no more than a few words with dozens of people—bank tellers, cab drivers, department-store clerks, doormen, waiters, grocery-store clerks, ticket takers, cashiers, flight attendants. We're usually so absorbed in our own thoughts that they become *nonpeople* to us. They are robots who open doors, take our tickets, swipe bar codes on our groceries, take our money, and give us change. Likewise, we are nonpeople to them. We are just one more customer to open a door for, take a ticket from, or swipe the bar codes for.

Whichever side of the counter you are on, here is a way to bring even more sunshine into both the stranger's day and yours. I call it *giving an eye message*, not an "I" message. After you've conducted your business, give the stranger an extra second or two of eye contact before looking away. He or she, feeling your eyes, will look up. You both will feel the pulse of electricity between you. It's like a flashing neon sign which reads, "We are really connecting and communicating. I think you are special."

♡More Magnetic Attraction!

As they go throughout their day, People Magnets miraculously transform *nonpeople* into VIPs with an extra moment of eye contact. They give the painter an extra pulse of the peepers. They give the seamstress an extra shot of the shutters. In an eye blink, they alter the encounter from ordinary business-as-usual into a special one. At the end of the day, the twinkles in their smiling eyes will probably have added up to less than one minute. But it makes a world of difference in how people respond to PMs.

When I was a flight attendant, I passed meal trays to thousands of passengers, only to hear back a mumbled "thank-you" which had the sincerity of a TV laugh track. Instantly inspecting the size of the meatloaf or counting the number of peas, they seemed oblivious to the fact that there was a human hand holding the tray. What a treat it was for me when the rare passenger looked me right in my eyes, smiled, and, unrushed and unmumbled, articulated, "Thank-you" or "Thank-you, you're doing a great job." (How much do you want to bet I gave *that* passenger priority service for the rest of the flight?)

I'm sure you've had that same empty feeling when, making a purchase at a drugstore, the sales clerk placed the change in your hand and never did her eyes meet yours. Here you could have been the abominable snowman and, as long as the repository for the change, your hand, looked human, she would never have noticed.

Be sure to discharge a little blast of joy into everyone's life. Keeping your eyes on theirs for that transitory, fleeting second says so much. Translation:

I find you interesting.
I think you are attractive.
I like you.

We are on the same wavelength.
Our auras are touching.
It is a brief moment in both our lives,
   but we are both here, now.
I respect you.
You are a person to me.
You are special.

When you say thank-you to the cashier at lunch, give her an extra moment of lingering eye contact. When you say thank-you to the bus driver, give him an extra shot of eye contact. When you say thank-you to the bellhop who has carried your bag, give him an extra beat of eye contact. When you say thank-you to the dry-cleaning clerk who hands you your clothes, flash him an extra second of your gaze.

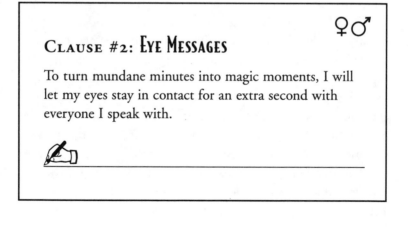

Clause #2: Eye Messages

To turn mundane minutes into magic moments, I will let my eyes stay in contact for an extra second with everyone I speak with.

7 Win Their Hearts, in Ten Words or Less

One of my duties, when I was a flight attendant, was to stand by the door as passengers were disembarking and wish each farewell. Now this presented a problem because saying good-bye more than a hundred times in a row gave the impression of a Barbie doll on one triple A battery.

In order to avoid this, I determined that my voice, when speaking at a low to normal tone in a crowd, carried about twelve feet. I then calculated that five passengers in a row with all their carry-on luggage covered that twelve feet. Ergo, the sixth impatient passenger couldn't hear me. Quick arithmetic on the fingers of one hand told me I should prepare five different good-byes so no passenger felt he or she was getting a canned one. My riff simply became, "Good-bye," "So long," "Good-bye, I hope you enjoyed your flight," and, depending on our destination, a "Cheerio," "Adios," "Ciao," "Sayonara," or "Auf Wiedersehen."

To my surprise, only one of the farewells above brought sincere smiles, not the fake ones that people who have been squashed in narrow seats and turning the other cheek for eight hours give. Can you guess which one it was?

The *sincere* smiles came from the folks to whom I said, "Good-bye, I hope you enjoyed your flight" which I call "the

♡ More Magnetic Attraction!

When People Magnets say "thank-you," they give the pleasure that the word intends by explaining *why* they are thankful. They give every thank-you a little padding. Big smiles are always the PMs reward.

expanded thank-you." When I felt the warm response, I started expanding or specifying all my thank-yous to people, on the plane and off.

The expanded thank-yous also help us wriggle out of those unpleasant little predicaments we find ourselves in every day. Just last week when I was buying a lipstick, a cosmetics sales clerk waited patiently as I vascillated between the cardinal red, the crimson red, the coral red, the ruby red, the scarlet red, or the vermilion red. Finally, much to her relief, I made a decision. Upon parting, I said, "Thanks for your patience with my indecision." She gave a big smile and lied, "Oh no, it was no problem. I know how important it is to get just the right color."

♀♂ Clause #3: The Expanded Thank-You

Before saying thank-you, I will think to see if it fits to tell *why* I am thankful. Then I'll say, "Thanks for . . ."

 _____

---

8 The Magic Wand, Your Body

The potency of human physical contact is powerful. When two bodies touch, you can actually feel the energy oozing out of one and flowing into the other.

A handshake, a hug, even an embrace between people, especially strangers, must follow convention. You can shake hands with a stranger when introduced. You can hug a stranger at a ball game when your team has won. You can even embrace a stranger if you have both suffered a grievous loss. Grief counselors at airports after a crash use the embrace to console as often as they use words.

One kind of touch between strangers, however, is not regulated. In fact, it is so fast, so fleeting, you're not even sure it happened. In fact, it *must* be so brisk that no one could mistake its intent, especially if coming from a man. This is the accidental or trifling touch.

It can be hands touching when exchanging money, or shoulders brushing on the bus. The imperceptible flash of electricity between you is fleeting, yet forceful enough to create warmth.[13] It is saying, "I accept you. You are not, like the ancient lowest caste in India, untouchable."

More Magnetic Attraction!

It is transitory, yet it contains the potency of an embrace. It is ephemeral, yet it invokes strong subconscious emotions. People Magnets use the trifling touch tastefully and judiciously to create a subconscious excitement between them and the people they touch.

It can also be a longer light touch on the shoulder instead of a tap when you want to get someone's attention.

Several months ago, I was taking the last train home from Boston and was in a deep sleep. As the train pulled into Penn station in New York, I slowly and happily came out of dreamland. When I was fully conscious, I looked up into the beautiful dark, kind, face of the conductor. He had his hand on my shoulder and was shaking me ever so gently, as he said, "Here we are, ma'am. New York City. End of the line. Did you sleep well?"

I suppose some might think his lengthy touch was inappropriate, but I knew it came from a good heart and nothing else. I'm sure he would have awakened a male passenger with the same tender touch.

How much better it was than many pokings, jabbings, nudgings, proddings, or loudmouthed, touchless "Ma'am wake up"s I'd received on various trains, planes, and buses over the years.

One cautionary note: women can use this trifling touch more securely than men. Due to our increased awareness of sexual harassment, men must be more prudent. However, if done in good taste with no questionable motives, men may also spread sunshine with the trifling touch.

♀♂

CLAUSE #4: THE TRIFLING TOUCH

I will try to find appropriate occasions to allow my hand or shoulder to fleetingly touch another's. It is like a quick-as-a-wink caress. Rather than tapping someone on the shoulder to get attention, *if appropriate*, I will apply a longer, gentler, kinder, tender touch.

 _____

9 Like Hallmark Cards, a Smile for Every Occasion

I was once patiently awaiting my appointment in the doctor's waiting room with four or five other patients. There was a cantankerous, crabby old curmudgeon of a man who grumbled to the nurse each time she came in for the next patient. I would have placed my bets that he hadn't smiled in a year.

While he was sitting there grumbling to himself, a woman with an adorable six-month-old baby came in and sat across from him. Everyone looked at the woman and smiled, but not crusty old crab.

After a few minutes when everyone had gone back to their reading, I saw the baby giving the grouchy old guy a big toothless grin that seemed to be for him and him alone. How long do you think the old sourpuss held out not smiling? Not two seconds. He cracked a smile that threatened to fracture his face from ear to ear. When the nurse came to get me for my appointment, he didn't growl at her. He was still smiling like the first spring flower after a long cold winter and cooing, "Well, hello, there little feller."

So what warranted this exceptional reaction? Was it that the baby was so cute? Perhaps that's part of it. But mainly it was because the baby's smile was not quick and plastic. It was slow, flooding, and *genuine*. It was not the stretched professional smile

> ## ♡More Magnetic Attraction!
>
> The most obvious difference between a real smile and a sincere smile is *timing*. People Magnets' smiles are slow, really slow. They flood over their faces. They seem to well up from somewhere inside their hearts and when their hearts are just too full from enjoying what their eyes behold, it spills out into a smile. A PM's smile says, "Wow, I really like what I see."

of the travel agent or ticket taker. It was not the quick-flash ingratiating smile of the beggar or the bellhop. It was not the bluffing frozen smile of the negotiator, or the conniving smile of the used-car dealer. It was a slow flooding sincere just-for-you-because-I-like-looking-at-your-face smile.

Nobody told the little tyke, "Now be sure to smile at strangers, especially ugly old crabs like the one who is sitting in the doctor's office." The baby obviously didn't see a cranky disagreeable old man. He saw something he liked in the old crab's face. And that's what we can do too. See the beauty in everyone's face (it really is there if you look hard enough!). Smile at that.

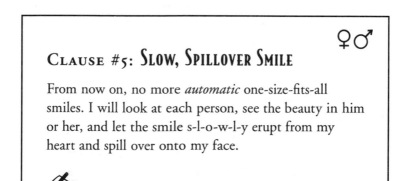

♀♂

Clause #5: Slow, Spillover Smile

From now on, no more *automatic* one-size-fits-all smiles. I will look at each person, see the beauty in him or her, and let the smile s-l-o-w-l-y erupt from my heart and spill over onto my face.

10 Why Do We Prefer One Person Over Another?

Several years ago I was helping my friend Deborah pack up her linens and dishes because she, her husband Tony, and their two daughters, aged four and five were moving from New York City to San Francisco. Deborah was telling me she was worried Julie and Lucy might not fit in with the kids there.

"Deborah," I said, "You've got to be kidding. You think the girls are going to go up to another kid and, in a real New Yawk accent, say, 'Shaddup schnook.'"

"No," she protested. "I mean, they're used to being well liked. All the kids in their nursery school enjoy playing with them, and now they have to start all over."

"Start all over?" I asked with a touch of friendly mockery. "I see, like politicians winning over a new constituency?"

"Well, sort of," she replied. "I've worked very hard to give them the skills that make other kids want to play with them. In San Francisco, they'll be starting from ground zero again."

"You mean you gave them a course in Popularity 101."

"Well, I guess you could call it that," Deborah replied.

I chuckled, shook my head, and took a few more dishes off the shelf to wrap. How could tots Julie's and Lucy's age care if they played with one kid or another? What qualities could a well-liked tot have that a not-so-well-liked one didn't? At that tender age, I thought, they certainly couldn't have clearly defined personalities. Or could they?

I figured this was just another of Deborah's fads. She'd been through them all—Rolfing, Tantra, the Alexander technique, the Feldenkrais method, and when she got pregnant, she had Tony going to some New Age fathering classes.

"Impossible," I muttered to myself. Deborah obviously heard me because she said, "Leil, I'm not kidding. I have given the girls the most important skill they need to make friends."

"You mean they can tell jokes better than the other kids?" I asked. "I can just hear their comedy routine now. Lucy will go up to another kid and say, 'Hey, didja know my big sister Julie is so dumb she has to take off her shoes to count to twenty.' Then Julie will pipe up, 'Yeah, when she grows up they're going to use my sister as a mold for making dumbbells.' " Tastelessly, I chuckled at my own depraved humor.

"Stop it, Leil!" Deborah said. "I'm serious. Can you guess what one learned skill makes them more popular?"

"Listening."

"Sort of," Deborah said, "but it has nothing to do with hearing."

"I give up."

That was all the invitation she needed. Deborah went diving into a box of books she had already packed and pulled out a copy of the *Journal of Genetic Psychology*. Opening it to a dogeared page, she handed me the journal and commanded me: "Read!"

I looked at the unwieldy title, "The Association of Children's Nonverbal Decoding Abilities with Their Popularity, Locus of Control, and Academic Achievement."[14]

"What does *that* mean?" I asked.

"That means, in plain English for you Leil," she said, "that the better my girls are at reading other people's emotions by their nonverbal signals and tones of voice, the more well liked they'll be. I've taught the girls to watch whoever is speaking very carefully and respond first to their body language. That's the most important. Then comes responding to the sound of their voice, and only finally their words. Most people get it backward.

The study fascinated me because I knew that we receive information in just that order. Fifty percent is visual, 30 percent is sound, and only 20 percent comes from someone's actual words.

Deborah then told me how she had trained the girls to be little experts at this. Every evening she played a game called "Guess How I Feel?" Deborah would make a movement like rubbing her neck or wringing her hands and the girls would identify it. Each time they played "Guess How I Feel?" the signals got more subtle.

They also played a game called "Truth or Lies?" where, for example, Deborah would put her hand to her mouth or fidget while telling them a story. She would then ask the girls whether they thought she was telling the truth or not. (Hand over the mouth is a common signal of lying.)

Still skeptical, I said, "Oh, come on Deborah, I was expecting something a bit more scientific from you. You know, some psychology—Jungian, Adlerian, or Freudian at least."

"You don't think it will work?" she asked.

"I'll eat my hat if it does," I responded.

Deborah Gets the Last Laugh (and Leil Eats Her Hat)

The next year, on what has now become my annual visit to Deborah and Tony's in San Francisco, was Deborah's year for Pilates, an exercise regime where you work out on a machine that looks like an ancient torture rack.

One afternoon her class ran late so she asked me to pick up the girls at kindergarten. When I arrived at the school, the principal invited me to come to the playroom and get them. As we walked down the hall, she was gushing about the girls. "Everyone loves Julie and Lucy. They're such nice girls, and so smart!"

We entered a large classroom where about thirty-five children were running in circles, jumping, laughing, and tossing toys all over. Lucy was sitting in a large circle with about a dozen other

♡ MORE MAGNETIC ATTRACTION!

People Magnets listen with their hearts by watching people carefully to see how they *feel* about what they are saying. PMs *listen* to their gestures, *listen* to their fidgeting, *listen* to their skin flushing, *listen* to their eye contact, and *listen* to everything else they can see about the person who is talking.

kids who were playing a game similar to an old TV game show called "To Tell the Truth," except the kids formed two teams, the "telling team" and the "guessing team."

One kid on the telling team named Sally started by saying, "My parents promised to take me to Disneyland for my birthday this year." The next kid, Willie, said, "My parents promised to take me to Disneyland for my birthday this year." And so on down the line, each said, "My parents promised to take me to Disneyland for my birthday this year." I couldn't help but notice Lucy. The other kids were listening to the speaker, but Lucy's eyes were glued to the speaker.

Just as the final kid, Jason, finished saying, "My parents promised to take me to Disneyland for my birthday this year," Lucy piped up with, "Willie is the *real* one."

Willie nodded in confirmation. "Hooray! Hooray!" Everyone started clapping. The wide-eyed principal leaned over to me and said, "I just don't know how she does it. It's truly phenomenal. She guesses right almost every time. Just hearing one sentence, she knows who's telling the truth. It's almost eerie."

I agreed that it was indeed phenomenal. However, I knew little Lucy had no mystical or supernatural powers. Deborah had told me the secret.

As I was helping Julie on with her coat, I overheard Lucy talking with Willie.

"When are you going to go to Disneyland?"

Little Willie with downcast eyes said, "Next month."

Lucy obviously knew something was wrong. "You don't wanna go?" she asked.

"I wanna go, but . . ." Willie, still looking down, started digging his toe into the floor.

Like the most exquisitely trained psychiatrist, Lucy didn't say anything. She just kept looking peacefully and sympathetically at Willie. "It's just that," Willie continued hesitantly, "I'm going alone with just my Dad because, he and Mom, well my Dad moved out last month and . . ."

Lucy put her hand on little Willie's arm, looked right into his eyes, and neither kid needed to say another word. No wonder all the kids loved Lucy. She knew how to listen with her heart more than her ears.

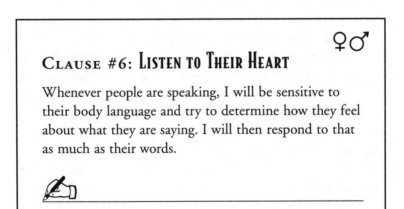

Clause #6: Listen to Their Heart

Whenever people are speaking, I will be sensitive to their body language and try to determine how they feel about what they are saying. I will then respond to that as much as their words.

11 ♡ Fine Tuning Your Tongue

The second language lesson I learned from Dale came as a bomb-shell, especially coming from a guy who cut his teeth on a gun barrel. On his last business trip to New York, we decided to meet for lunch. I arrived at the restaurant a bit early and waited five minutes, ten. Just as it was coming up on fifteen, I spotted his big ten-gallon hat hovering above the crowd like a flying saucer. He handed it to a beaming hatcheck attendant who pretended she needed help from another to carry it.

When he reached the table, he said, "Oh, I bet you were about to send the bloodhounds out for me. But don't you worry little lady, ol' Dale knows how to take care of himself, even in Noo Yawk City."

Dale said, "I'm as hungry as a goat on a concrete pasture, how about you?" A minute later, while looking at our menus, he peeked sheepishly over his and said, "I hope you weren't offended by what I just said."

"The goat?" I asked sincerely.

"No, that 'little lady' bit. I durn near got my mouth washed out with soap last week at the office. And all I said was 'the switch-board gal' was sick that day. Well, my right-hand gal, er person, Stephanie, set me straight."

This piqued my curiosity, and I asked him to tell me more. He said, "Well, I knew my tongue was as wild as an unbroken bronco and it needed some ropin'. So I took her to lunch and she told me a slew of things."

"Like what?"

"Like I wouldn't say 'my lawyer guy' or 'accountant guy' so why say 'switchboard gal?' I should've said 'switchboard operator.' Then she said if I were going to refer to a female, I should say 'woman,' not 'gal' or 'girl' or 'lady.'" He thought for a second and then said, "So I guess that means 'little lady' is out too?"

"Well, yes, Dale, it does," I said. "But if you can prove with a birth certificate and residency papers that you were born and bred in Texas, people will forgive you."

"Whoa, Miss Leil, I say a mighty big thank-you to that. But I don't deserve any excuses. My body may be in the second millennium, but my mouth is still in the first. No, this ol' Lone Star feller has to change his ways when it comes to the uh, 'other-but-equal' sex.

"Stephanie suggested a couple of good books for me to read. I told her, 'I sure would like to read 'em, but I know I'm not going to find the time.' I asked her if she would write me a little crib sheet to make me poh-litically correct." Here Dale reached into his pocket and pulled out an obviously well-studied, dog-eared piece of paper. "Here's the inventory of tricks I'm trying to train my tongue to do," he said.

It just so happened I also had a written list of linguistic dos and don'ts in my purse that day because my tongue too was lagging behind my awareness.

Dale and I swapped our lists and simultaneously cracked up. Practically all of his *don't say* list for men was on my *do say* list for women, and vice versa.

I asked Dale if I could borrow his list and present it here.

"Why, sure, little lady, er I mean Leil, that would be an honor."

Gentlemen, follow these rules and 90 percent of the ammunition in the workplace war between the sexes will be demolished. Innocent female employees will no longer feel ravaged and pillaged. You will no longer be accused of dictatorial tactics. And the office battle of the sexes may soon take its place in ancient history along side of the Battle of Hastings or the Seven Years War.

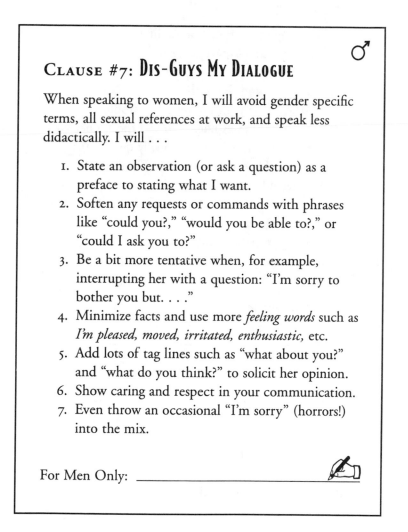

CLAUSE #7: DIS-GUYS MY DIALOGUE

When speaking to women, I will avoid gender specific terms, all sexual references at work, and speak less didactically. I will . . .

1. State an observation (or ask a question) as a preface to stating what I want.
2. Soften any requests or commands with phrases like "could you?," "would you be able to?," or "could I ask you to?"
3. Be a bit more tentative when, for example, interrupting her with a question: "I'm sorry to bother you but. . . ."
4. Minimize facts and use more *feeling words* such as *I'm pleased, moved, irritated, enthusiastic,* etc.
5. Add lots of tag lines such as "what about you?" and "what do you think?" to solicit her opinion.
6. Show caring and respect in your communication.
7. Even throw an occasional "I'm sorry" (horrors!) into the mix.

For Men Only: _____

Women, here is your part of the peace treaty. When you follow these seven simple rules, your male colleagues, friends, and sweethearts will actually understand you, and you'll go up a notch in their estimation.

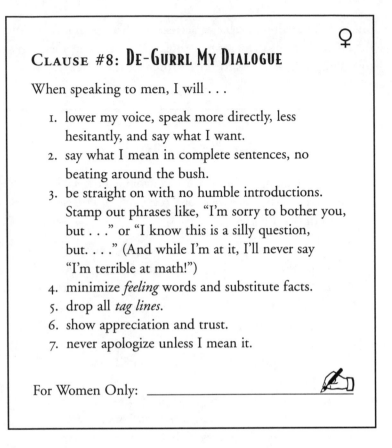

♀

Clause #8: De-Gurrl My Dialogue

When speaking to men, I will . . .

1. lower my voice, speak more directly, less hesitantly, and say what I want.
2. say what I mean in complete sentences, no beating around the bush.
3. be straight on with no humble introductions. Stamp out phrases like, "I'm sorry to bother you, but . . ." or "I know this is a silly question, but. . . ." (And while I'm at it, I'll never say "I'm terrible at math!")
4. minimize *feeling* words and substitute facts.
5. drop all *tag lines*.
6. show appreciation and trust.
7. never apologize unless I mean it.

For Women Only: _____

I knew Dale saw the folly of his ways and genuinely planned to change. I told him, however, that I hope he didn't change his Texas charm.

"Yep," he said. "I've been told I could charm the knickers off the queen mother."

Old habits are hard to break.

12 Never Hear "You're Not Listening!" Again

Have you ever talked to a nail sticking out of wood? It doesn't nod. It doesn't say "Uh huh." It seldom smiles. It just stands there until you have finished speaking. Gentlemen, with all due respect, you listen like a nail—which, when listening to other men, is great. That's how you've been taught to listen. That's how to signal to other men that you are listening. However, if you listen that way to a woman, she'll want to take a hammer, give the nail (you) a thwack on the head, and scream, "Why aren't you listening?"

Last year I spoke at a terrific women's leadership conference in Mexico which was attended by several hundred women and half a dozen brave husbands or significant others who had come along for the sun and the beaches.[15] About ten concurrent sessions for women and one for men on subjects ranging from entrepreneurial to spiritual ran at any one time. I attended a variety of seminars but, on the last day, the one that caught my eye was for men and was called "Living With a Successful Woman."

Totally inappropriate, of course, for me to attend, so I asked the facilitator if I would be able to purchase the recording. Alas, no arrangements had been made—I was guessing the men didn't want their wives or *significant others* to hear all that male bonding and female bashing. (I later discovered there was none of the

♡ More Magnetic Attraction!

A picture of a male listening is definitely a still life.
A picture of a woman listening is high animation.
When PMs want the other sex to stop saying, "You
never listen to me," they simply practice cross-gender
listening.

latter—just the opposite. This remarkable muster of males was
very proud of their successful wives. As one man said, "Especially
when I look at the monthly bank statement of our joint account.")

The facilitator generously invited me to attend, and I
accepted, but only if the participants had no objections and I
could be a "fly on the wall." However, so my presence wouldn't
inhibit the men, I sat behind a big screen where I could hear but
would not be seen.

At the beginning of the session, the facilitator suggested each
man introduce himself and tell about his successful partner and
their relationship. The first man started speaking . . . and speaking . . . and speaking. He must have gone on for about ten minutes, and I began to wonder if the other men had left because I
heard nothing. No "uh huh," no comments, no questions, no
nothing. Had they walked out?

But, no. It soon became evident that each man was speaking
in turn, and those constant little noises that we women make to
show our support of the speaker were conspicuously absent in
their dialogue. Or, I should say, during each man's monologue.

Holy mackerel! I thought, this is unusual. I was so surprised
by the phenomenon that, after the conference, when I returned to
my office, I combed through a batch of studies on male/female listening. Some pretty eye-opening results.

We think women are better listeners? No way! We just listen
differently. We constantly nod to let the speaker know we are listening. We make supportive noises to confirm that we under-

stand what is being said. Until that moment, I didn't consider my innocent way of overlapping supportive statements to be interruptions. But many men would! Be careful, sisters. We have to adopt a different listening demeanor around men. (As men should when speaking with us.)

Conversely, men only nod when they agree with the speaker. They might argue that the male way of listening is superior because it isn't about momentary responses.

We think women talk more than men? Again, no way! Men talk much more than women at work. For them, talking is a form of competing and getting their ideas across. When they're at home, their silence simply means they're taking a vacation from having to compete.

Women interrupt each other more in a noncompetitive way. It is mainly to jump in with their own encouraging statements.[16] Like those little plastic ducks that bob up and down into a glass, we are constantly nodding our head. All that says is, "I understand what you're saying."

Incidentally, when it comes to language, what's good for the Western goose may not be good for the Eastern gander. For instance, if you're traveling to the Far East, toss linguistic advice over the Japanese screen or, at least, take it with a splash of teriyaki sauce. Say you're an American mother and you come upon your kid in the kitchen gleefully taking raw eggs from the refrigerator and dropping them one by one on the floor. "Whee!" Plop. "Whee!" Plop. Naturally, you'd go berserk and, at the very least, say, "No, stop!"

The Japanese mother, on the other hand, feels saying "no" means losing status. Discussion means gaining status and harmony.[17] So the Japanese mom says to her little tyke, "Oh, isn't that interesting. Who drops eggs on the floor, Kieko? Do you know anyone who drops eggs on the floor? Have you ever seen anyone dropping eggs on the floor? Mr. Egg is saying 'Ouch.'"

In fact a Japanese gentleman named Ueda wrote a paper called "Sixteen Ways to Avoid Saying 'No' in Japan"—and this guy was serious![18]

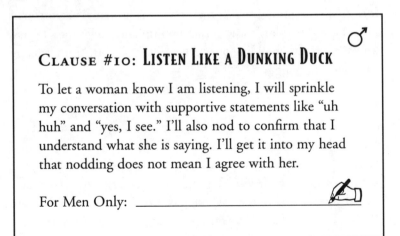

Clause #9: Listen Like a Nail

When speaking with a man, I will cut the constant nodding and little supporters like "uh huh," "yes," "oh," and other *cooing* noises. He'll think I'm interrupting! (Imagine that.) I will get it into my head that if I just stand looking at him while he speaks, he'll think I'm a great listener.

For Women Only: _____

Clause #10: Listen Like a Dunking Duck

To let a woman know I am listening, I will sprinkle my conversation with supportive statements like "uh huh" and "yes, I see." I'll also nod to confirm that I understand what she is saying. I'll get it into my head that nodding does not mean I agree with her.

For Men Only: _____

13 Fragging the Fatal FUD Factor

There may be some differences in thinking between the Orient and the Occident, but one idea is universal. We must have confidence if we hope to win at any game, be it athletic, business, social, or romantic.

Olympic athletes, performance artists, and even business people who want to always be at their best are turning increasingly to sports psychologists. I have the good fortune to know a sports psychologist named Stan who, with one simple technique, made a great difference in my life.

We were having a quick lunch in a coffee shop one day when he told me he was working with a Japanese Olympic skater whose name he asked me not to use—we'll call her Tseuko. He said she had all the talent and skill she needed to get the gold medal. Nevertheless, she lacked confidence in herself—a fatal flaw in athletes, as in all of us. (When reporters asked her, "Will you win?" her answer was, "I'm going to try." Not good enough, Tseuko!) Stan told me that unless you truly know in the depth of your heart that you are a winner, you never will be. You have to believe it constantly—not just while competing—but while sleeping, eating, showering, talking, and partying. Stan calls that constant assurance being in *the zone*.

But What About Me?
I'm No Olympic Athlete

I asked him whether finding *the zone*, as he called it, would work for the rest of us who were not going for a gold medal.

"What do you mean?" he asked. "We're all going for the gold. Maybe not a gold medal for ice skating, skiing, or track, still, we're going for the gold in our jobs, in dealing with our families. We're going for the gold in making friends and finding love, or making love last. Everyone's definition of *gold* is different, but the method of getting it is the same. You get in *the zone*, or you wind up like a pancake on ice."

I asked him, "So where is this *zone* place?"

He said, "For some people it's right in their own backyard. For others it's very far away and takes very long to get to."

My next question was, of course, "Well, how far is it for me?"

"I don't know," he answered, "but if you like, we can find out. Let me ask you to do the same thing I asked Tseuko." Stan drew the following sketch on a napkin.

"Now," he said, "on the five lines, write the five people you talk with the most in your life. If you have more than five whom you deal with every day, you can add more lines and put the same letters beside the lines."

Before continuing to read, please do the same. List five people you know and who know you pretty well. They can be same sex friends, other sex friends, lovers, brothers, sisters, a spouse or significant other—someone who you feel has an influence on you. For now, ignore the letters beside the lines and just write the names. We'll return to the exercise in a moment.

Lack of confidence had eliminated Tseuko the year before, and now Stan had only three months to work with her and make her honestly feel "I am the best." This was his number one tough challenge because Tseuko had grown up in Japan where the joyful arrogance and good-natured bantering and boasting so widespread in American sportsmanship was nonexistent. A Japanese motto, translated, says, "The nail that stands out must be hammered down."

To make matters worse, Tseuko was romantically involved with a man who, out of his own insecurity, belittled Tseuko. The number two challenge Stan faced was showing Tseuko how boyfriend, Akiro, was sabotaging her self image. Only if he could accomplish this, could he go for the goal—qualifying Tseuko to go for the gold.

The five people Tseuko wrote on her list were her mother and her father in Kyoto, whom she spoke with every day on the phone; her sister who lived in the States; then there was her best friend, an American girl named Jenny; and, of course, her boyfriend Akiro.

Stan asked Tseuko to think about her conversations with each person on her list and to circle the set of initials which most accurately described how much, if any, they criticized her.

Before continuing to read, please do the same. Circle CN if the person whose name is on that line "never" criticizes you. Circle CS if he or she "seldom" criticizes you. CB is an interesting one; it stands for criticizes "beneficially." Circle that if, at times, that person does criticize you, but it has a positive effect. You feel that person gives criticism without rancor, and it helps you grow.

Mark CL if the person on that line criticizes you a "lot," and CA if he or she is "always" criticizing you.

Tseuko's list looked like this: her mother and sister, CN; her father, CS; her girlfriend Jenny, CB; and her boyfriend Akiro,

CA. (My list was almost identical two CNs, a CS, a CB, and one CA.)

Stan's first step in helping Tseuko get in *the zone* was to get her talking about herself, her life in Japan, her new life as an Olympic athlete, her training, and her relationships. Throughout her narrative, he interjected questions about her feelings. "How do you feel when your sister is watching, and you skate really well? How do you feel when your friend Jenny is watching and you skate really well?"

Stan noticed that whenever Tseuko talked about her family who was so proud of her, her back straightened, her deep brown eyes sparkled, and a soft confident smile framed her lips. This was the feeling Stan needed Tseuko to have always. Conversely, whenever Tseuko talked about her boyfriend, her shoulders tensed up and her eyes fell.

Then he asked Tseuko the million-dollar question, the one that, when Tseuko tried to answer, caused her to break into tears. That question was, "How do you *feel* when your boyfriend is watching and you skate really well?"

Tseuko realized, at that moment, that she had never skated well when Akiro was watching.

How You Can Go for the Gold

Now go back to your list. If all of your relationships are CSs (criticizes seldom) or CNs (criticizes never) you are very fortunate indeed. Supportive people surround you. If you have any CBs on your list, make sure they are indeed criticizing only beneficially, and that you are genuinely growing and improving by their guidance. The problem comes if you find any CAs (criticizes always) or CLs (criticizes a lot). If you do, and you can eliminate them from your life or at least diminish your exposure to them, please do.

However, if you want or need to keep a relationship with someone who criticizes you a lot—we'll call this person a "Trasher"—you must get him or her to stop reproaching you.

That is if you are going to be successful in stamping out Fear, Uncertainty, and Doubt (FUD). You can't feel good about yourself if someone important to you is constantly gnawing away at your self-esteem.

You must take the Trasher aside and explain how it makes you feel when he or she criticizes you. Be very specific. Describe your symptoms. Describe the result. For example, you might say, "George, I know you think you are telling me this for my own good. Nevertheless, every time you criticize me, I get short of breath; my heart beats faster; I begin to feel worthless; and then later I find myself getting angry. I don't want this to happen. You are too important to me."

You must also decide on an ultimatum if the criticism continues. Depending on your relationship, this can be as light as walking out of the room or out of the house—or as strong as walking out of that person's life.

Obviously you can't walk out on your parents or a spouse in an otherwise good marriage, especially if you have children. Choose your ultimatum carefully because, when the nonbeneficial criticism starts, you must stick with it.

The tale of Tseuko has a happy ending. In the weeks that followed, she and Stan spoke more about her relationship with

♥More Magnetic Attraction!

The reason why juries are sequestered in trials is so they won't be influenced by the media or what their friends or family say. It's the same here. PMs know you can't have contact with people who are constantly criticizing you and still feel good about yourself. If these folks (we'll call them "Bitchers") are not crucial in your life for other reasons, well, they just gotta go! As my mother would say, "Give them their walking papers. Now!"

Akiro. It was Tseuko herself who came to the conclusion that she should sever the relationship. After that, her skating improved dramatically.

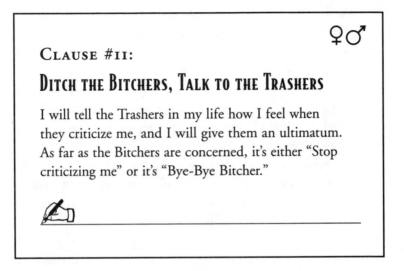

CLAUSE #11:

DITCH THE BITCHERS, TALK TO THE TRASHERS

I will tell the Trashers in my life how I feel when they criticize me, and I will give them an ultimatum. As far as the Bitchers are concerned, it's either "Stop criticizing me" or it's "Bye-Bye Bitcher."

14 Beauty Is as Beauty Feels

Nowadays, the old insult, "she's so thin, she has to wear snowshoes when she takes a shower" is a compliment. Many women would smile smugly overhearing this said about them. "You can never be too rich or too thin," they say. Thin is in, slender is splendor.

It seems no matter how good-looking someone is, everyone has a gripe about his or her own appearance. This is *not* the way to be a people magnet, as you'll see. And the biggest gripe is about weight.

Once, trying on clothes in the department store, I overheard two young women in the next cubicle complaining. Apparently unhappy with her image in the mirror, one griped, "What a Jelly Belly I am! Why can't I get rid of this paunch? Ohmygosh, do you think I'm pregnant?"

The other, equally displeased with the image staring back at her said, "Stop complaining. Ol' Thunder Thighs here can't even get these jeans on!"

I must admit my warped curiosity got the better of me and I lurked around the jeans department so I could get a gander at Jelly Belly and Ol' Thunder Thighs when they left. No one came out of the dressing rooms for about five minutes except two very attractive slender young girls who dejectedly put some size eight jeans back on the rack. As they left, I heard them commiserating on their failure to cram their *chunky trunks* into the tiny jeans. If I hadn't recognized their whining voices, I never would have dreamed those two willowy creatures were the complainers of moments ago.

Well, if nothing else, the desire to be slender is testimony to our country's affluence because, in impoverished societies, jelly bellies and thunder thighs are coveted measurements.[19] Women's rights activists should also be delighted at the girls' attitude because history shows a direct correlation between skinny-mania and women's control of economic resources.[20]

However, none of this will console Jelly Belly and Ol' Thunder Thighs when they sit in front of their TV tonight watching reruns of "Beverly Hills 90210" or "Melrose Place" and bemoaning how much skinnier stars Donna and Amanda are.

Why mention these two actresses instead of a myriad of other attractive but emaciated media women? Because a study, conducted in the years that the show was popular, proved a direct correlation between "Beverly Hills 90210" watchers and women's eating disorders such as anorexia nervosa and bulimia (binging, then purging through laxatives or the old unhealthy—not to men-

More Magnetic Attraction!

You don't need to go around posing all over the place or you'll look like just that, a posie. But you do need to start paying attention to how you *move*. Strong masculine movements are in. Have a good stride. Courteous movements are in. Stand up when she comes back from the ladies room to the restaurant table. Protective movements are in. Offer the lady your arm when you cross the street. Loving movements are in. Straighten her collar or adjust her hair after putting her coat on.

tion disgusting—finger-down-the-throat, weight-control home remedy).[21]

Women who watched "Seinfeld" and "Northern Exposure," other popular shows then that starred normal-weight women (Elaine and Maggie), suffered fewer eating disorders. Watchers of "Designing Women" and "Roseanne" starring a couple of heavy-weights (Suzanne and Roseanne) had fewer eating disorders still.

Does that mean that the shows were the cause of the disorders? I didn't think so. But in a similar study, researchers asked women which of three models they liked best: Kate Moss (thin), Cindy Crawford (average), or Anna Nicole Smith (heavy). This time there was an inverse proportion between the number of women suffering severe eating disorders and the number of pounds these models tipped the scales at.

I'm not entirely convinced, but the researchers decided that these findings proved that the thin media personalities were causing women to have eating disorders. This brings us to the weighty subject of this chapter.

First, medical professionals have proved, beyond all reasonable doubt, that today's exaggerated standards of thinness are not healthy. Also, between Kate Moss, Cindy Crawford, and Anna Nicole Smith, who do you think most males prefer? Cindy Crawford, of course. These and other observations convinced me that men like well-shaped women, not the ones who are so thin they don't have a shadow.

Think of the great sex symbols of yesteryear—Betty Grable, Marilyn Monroe, Lana Turner, Hedy Lamarr, Dorothy Lamour, Rosalind Russell, Carmen Miranda. Talk about Jelly Bellies! And if Dorothy Lamour ever got one of today's wrestlers in a headlock with her thighs, he'd never get up again.

Yes, men do like thin. In fact in an analysis of personal ads *thin* topped the list of twenty-eight qualities men sought in a potential date.[22] (*Financially secure* topped the women's wish list.) However, at this writing, men still prefer their women to be a little heavier than most extremely fashion-conscious females want to be. (Did you ever see protruding collar bones and rib cages in a pin-up calendar?) But, if we're not careful, the male interpretation of a *thin woman* will get dangerously close to a women's exaggerated, almost unattainable standard of thinness.

Furthermore, if men are beginning to appreciate a much thinner woman, it's our own (women's) darn fault. It seems, in the case of fashion, taste is on the curve, not the cusp, of the wave. To substantiate high fashion's influence on taste, a male researcher, Nigel Barber, wangled a foundation grant to study curvaceousness in women. (Another of those "Nice-work-if-you-can-get-it" assignments.)

Mr. Barber's study, which he called "Secular Changes in Standards of Bodily Attractiveness in American Women: Different Masculine and Feminine Ideals," contrasted the measurements of Miss America contestants and Playboy bunnies (a male's fantasy of *ideal women*) with measurements of Vogue models (more of a female view of *ideal women*).[23] He tracked the curves from about 1921 until 1986 when, owing to political pressure, the measurements of Miss America contestants became a secret as carefully guarded as the formula for Coca-Cola.

His findings? Generally, a female's vision of the *Ideal Woman* is getting thinner, and thinner, and thinner—and has far fewer curves than the male's erotic example of feminine pulchritude. Owing to female fashion editors (and perhaps some designers in the industry who are quite pleased that their curvaceousness is now rivaling the more boyish measurements of the top models) that is changing. The male concept of the ideal woman is, happily, still behind theirs. But as the calendar flips from year to year, the girls on it are becoming thinner too. Researchers speculate this is in response to the beauty images women are putting forth.

Incidentally, women, don't believe everything you see in a magazine regarding weight. I was once picking up some photos at a retoucher. John, the retoucher, was hovered over a photo. He said to his assistant, "If I airbrush any more, there's going to be nothing left of her." I peeked over his shoulder and saw a beautiful bikini-clad blonde with hardly any waist. I could tell from the opaque pigment around her belly that a good 10 percent of it had already been blown away and his airbrush was still spraying strong.

Thunder Thighs Wins Olympic Gold Medal for Love

As is so often the case, it's not the actual product, but how it is advertised that makes or breaks it. It's the same with people. You advertise yourself as beautiful, and you seem all the more so.

I was visiting my good friend Bonnie several months ago. Bonnie is no lightweight, either mentally or physically. In fact, she's pretty weighty in both departments.

We were sitting on the couch after dinner talking. The subject had turned to her happy marriage and I was joking that, if they gave an Olympic Gold Medal for how much your husband loved you, she would have no contenders.

Our conversation was interrupted by her husband who had just came back from a business trip. As if on cue to confirm my recent statement, the first thing he did was race over to the couch and scoop her up in his arms and say, "Hi Gorgeous." Now, if you know Bonnie's measurements, "scooping her up" was no mean feat. A few sarcastic unfeeling souls would say *he* should get the Gold Medal—for weight lifting. He gave Bonnie a big effusive loving kiss, paid his respects to me, and then excused himself to unpack.

I said, "Bonnie, how do you do it? How do you keep Tom so enraptured by you?" I hope that I did not, by the tone of my voice, insinuate "in spite of the fact that you're so overweight." However Bonnie must have understood that most people would have thought of the question in that light because she just laughed and, fluffing her hair in a mock gesture of *aren't I beautiful?*, said "Well, Tom just accepts my own opinion of myself and I guess I'm pretty narcissistic." As if to highlight that, she turned around several times, as gracefully as a model on a runway.

When we sat down again, we fell into a fascinating discussion. She told me she never makes any disparaging remarks about her own body. She has never asked Tom, "Honey do you think I'm too fat?" She always wears sexy underwear, sleeps in see-through teddies, and she told me, she even does sexy dances around the bedroom for Tom.

"You don't let him see your cellulite?" I asked in mock horror, grabbing the backs of my thighs to show her I was no stranger to that orange-peel-like puckering all women get on their legs.

Bonnie said, "Cellulite? You've got to be kidding. I once referred to those as my *dimples* and now Tom likes to nibble my *cute little dimples!*"

Bonnie is, of course dieting and exercising. She is working at weight loss as much as any overweight woman. The important thing is that, even before she sheds the pounds, she has pride in her own appearance. She loves her own body, and therefore Tom does too.

Do I hear you asking, "Does that mean I should be narcissistic? Yes, a little. If you're skeptical, please check out a study in the *Journal of Sex Research* on precisely this topic. It states that "Women's relationship status is directly related to their own subjective view of themselves and their sexual self-esteem, *not* to their actual body size or the objective researchers' rating of their physical attractiveness." In other words, if you feel beautiful and act like you are beautiful, it definitely magnifies your man's view of your beauty.[24]

Even more important, perhaps, than the echo-effect adoration you receive from him, is the effect that feeling beautiful has on your health. In an address to the medical community called

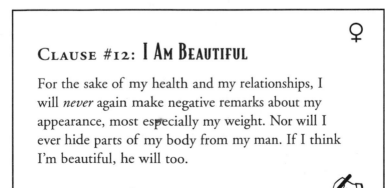

♀

Clause #12: I Am Beautiful

For the sake of my health and my relationships, I will *never* again make negative remarks about my appearance, most especially my weight. Nor will I ever hide parts of my body from my man. If I think I'm beautiful, he will too.

For Women Only: _____

"Psychosomatics of Beauty and Ugliness," the researchers gave evidence supported by doctors of medicine, psychiatry, psycho-analysis, and family therapy that, if you *feel* beautiful, you will be healthier and less apt to be ill.[25]

Gentlemen, lest you feel left out of the beauty game, don't! The same goes for you. The reason I write this clause for women is that you're not quite so hard on yourselves. Oh, sure, you occa-sionally check to make sure nobody is looking, then you turn sideways in the mirror to check to see if your contour is a bit more convex. Or you furtively hold a mirror up to the back of your head for a weekly inspection of how many hairs you've had to say "happy landing" to. But generally you pass muster when it comes to not complaining to your buddies or your women about your looks.

However, if you'd like to get a few more women whispering "he's soo handsome" when you pass the key is to—are you ready for this—become a *good mover.*

A good what? I'm sure you've seen the really cool dudes in the magazines advertising Calvin Klein undies or Armani jackets. They've got that intense "I can see right through your dress" look in their eyes and just enough five o'clock shadow to certify their manliness. The really cool part is the way they're standing, weight on one foot, jacket held by one finger and casually thrown over their right shoulder, and head cocked at just the right angle.

In the modeling business they're called *good movers.* And you can do it too.

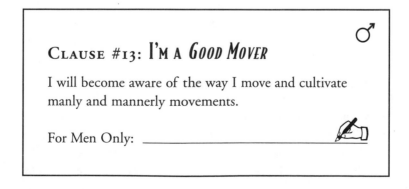

CLAUSE #13: I'M A *GOOD MOVER*

I will become aware of the way I move and cultivate manly and mannerly movements.

For Men Only: _____

15 How to Work a Room Like Royalty

Entering a room full of strangers is like jumping into an icy swimming pool. The worst part is standing on the edge, fearful of how it's going to feel when you smack against the water. But once you're in, it's not so cold after all, and you can start enjoying the swim.

You stand at the doorway of the party. Everyone is laughing, schmoozing, drinking, munching, and having such a good time. They all seem to know each other. Your knees are knocking together so loudly that you're sure in a minute they're all going to turn and look at you.

Here is how to avoid such upsetting episodes in your life. You're well armed with good eye contact, a sincere smile, and just the right handshake. You look good—except for that frozen look of sheer animal fear on your face. Naturally you want to replace it with a confident smile, but you would feel like a grinning idiot smiling at no one.

Here's the tactic. I call it "The Emperor's New Clothes." Perhaps you remember the story of the Emperor who was given a beautiful new suit of clothes that supposedly only the righteous could see. To all those who were not righteous, the suit would be invisible. Well, the Emperor made a proud procession through the streets and all of his subjects oohed and ahhed in admiration of the new suit. Naturally, they all wanted everybody else to think they were righteous and could see it. Until one honest little kid shouted, "But the king has on nothing at all!"

For this tactic, you will need an imaginary suit, but don't worry, you don't need to get naked.

Step One: As you stand at the door of the party, let your eyes settle on an empty space between several people on the far side of the room. Give the empty spot a big warm smile and a wave. You mustn't be concerned that you're beaming at a barren spot of wallpaper. The person to the right and left of it probably won't even notice, and, if they do, they won't look to see who you're smiling at.

If you do know someone on the other side of the room, all the better. But, even if they are facing the other direction, grace their posteriors with the same warm greeting you'd give their beckoning faces.

Step Two: Now you start your regal procession of one through the gathering. Think Queen Elizabeth. Think presidential candidates and "I want your vote." As you make your way through the throng of your subjects, give a smile, a nod, and small acknowledgment to every third or fourth person as you pass.

Will they know you're faking it? Absolutely not. Everyone else's insecurity will be in high gear and they'll think you know everybody. Those strangers you've smiled and nodded to will assume all the others were *real* acquaintances and you must have just mistaken them for someone else. Either that or you're a really famous person and, after all, *noblesse oblige* (the noble are obligated to acknowledge their court).

If you come upon someone you really do know, you're in luck. Now you can stop and chat a while. They'll feel lucky that, out of all the people you know at the party, you chose them to exchange a few words with.

Now you're in the pool. You can either tread water with a found acquaintance, or keep the breast stroke up until. . . .

Step Three: You catch up with your imaginary friends at the far end. "Hmm, where did they go?" Oh well, by now you have made a favorable impression on everyone you have acknowledged and on everyone who was merely watching you. So you take the last and final step of the procession.

Step Four: You look for someone to introduce yourself to. Another party goer standing alone is an excellent candidate. This loner has probably noticed you gliding confidently through the crowd greeting all your fans so he or she will be honored that you chose to stop and talk.

No solo souls standing around? Then head for the bar or the table of hors d'oeuvres where you'll find plenty of humans lurking. The food is not only fodder for feeding the folks, it's fodder for conversation with anyone else grazing at the trough.

"Hi, those carrot sticks look healthy, don't they? But I'm not in a healthy mood. Have you tried any of the other goodies yet?"

"Hello, think they'd laugh if I ask for a rum and coke?"

Incidentally, if you can refrain from holding something in your hands, do. Open arms make you more approachable and your hands are free for shaking other hands.

You may feel a tad silly the first time you use this technique but I have used it for years and have suggested it to many friends who swear by it. Happily, not one of us has ever encountered a kid like the one who told the hypocritical spectators, "The king is really naked!" Nobody's going to shout, "Ha ha, she's really bluffing and doesn't know anybody here."

Clause #14: The Emperor's New Clothes ♀♂

Whenever I enter a room where I don't know anyone,
I will spot imaginary friends on the other side of
the room and begin a regal glide toward them,
acknowledging every third or fourth "old acquaintance"
as I pass. Upon reaching my mark, I will strike up a
conversation with another "stand alone" (who will feel
honored that someone obviously so well connected
as I should grace them with my attention!).

16 Nice Shake!

Now we get into the realm of the first highly choreographed human contact, the handshake. In some societies, a handshake is more valid than a twenty-page contract. For example, in the diamond district of New York, countless millions of dollars of precious gems are bought, sold, and traded not on a contract, but a handshake. You break a contract and they can sue you. But you break the trust of a handshake and they break your kneecaps. And that's just for starters!

But let's talk about the tiny *contract* between any two people who shake hands. It reads, "Hello, I am open to a minute or two of conversation with you to see if we interest each other."

You extend your hand in friendship, and the first moments your epidermis touches that of a new person you are emitting—and receiving—thousands of subliminal signals. A handful of limp linguine whispers falteringly to your new acquaintance, "I am a passive loser with no people skills, and furthermore I am not the least bit interested in meeting you." The opposite isn't much better. The power crunch shouts in your new acquaintance's ear, "I'm really a wimp inside and I'm gonna try to prove I'm not by squeezing the bejesus out of your hand!"

Then there's "The Topper" who floats in from above expecting you to kiss his or her ring; "The Puller" who yanks you in so
suddenly you totter on your toes; "The Rifler" who extends his
arm so straight out that you want to raise your arms and beg
"Don't shoot!"; and, of course, the "Two-Handed Shaker" who,
no matter what he says next, you know he's after your vote, your
money, or your body.

The handshake that gives me the most pain to talk about is
the "Cold Wet Paw" because, though decades have passed, I will
never forget my anxious high-school years as a mushy mitt shaker.
At the first sign of nervousness, I didn't break out in uncontrol-
lable zits like many of my more fortunate friends. They could
cover their embarrassment with a dab of make-up. There was
nothing I could do about my cold, wet flippers. I tried everything
from little white lies about my sore hand, to pretending I didn't
see their hand suspended in the space between us in expectation
of mine joining it for a second or two of good fellowship. I
resorted to carrying a handkerchief and doing a quick swipe
before each shake. But this was to no avail. The swipe was too
obvious, and the hand too moist. My palms were a permanent perspiration factory.

Every June our school had what was called "The Best Of . . ."
award ceremony. An award was presented in the auditorium to the
best athlete and the student who had the best painting in art class,
the best science project, and the best essay in creative writing
class. I was to be the proud recipient of this last.

The joy of my magnificent moment was marred by fantasies
of extending my wet paw in front of the whole school. I prayed
the presenter's—and my—suffering would be brief.

When the big day arrived, I had made careful preparations to
reduce the disgrace. I was waiting with the other recipients in the
wings of the auditorium stage. Just as my name was called, I managed to unobtrusively give my hand a vigorous shake like a dog
emerging from the river, and next a final swipe on a hankie that
I then stashed in a backstage plant which, I am sure, welcomed
the moisture.

I strode proudly on stage and extended my right hand to Miss Lee, the presenter. Still clasping my right hand, she handed the award to me with her left. We both turned to the photographer who clicked. No flash. He clicked again. Nothing. Mumbling something about having to change his repeater bulb, he dove into his photo bag. Miss Lee let go of my hand which by now was starting to overflow with perspiration. During the two minutes it took the photographer to change bulbs, Miss Lee, sensing my shyness, gave the group a supportive little dialogue about the joys of creative writing. Little did she know that I was dying inside and that I felt beads of perspiration dripping from my hands in a fairly even flow now and forming a little puddle on the floor.

Ah, the photographer was ready. Miss Lee straightened up; repeated, "Congratulations, Leilie"; and she picked up the plaque. There was no circumventing the dreaded moment now. I couldn't tell her I'd just sprained my wrist in the past two minutes. Or that I suddenly decided I was going to become a surgeon or maybe a concert pianist, therefore I couldn't let mere mortals touch my hands.

With a big smile, she offered her right. I stared at it, frozen in fear. I didn't dare let nice Miss Lee clasp the cold wet fish I was hiding behind my back. A few seconds, which felt like hours, must have passed, because I heard the audience tittering. I had no recourse but to put my icy wet paw into Miss Lee's warm arid hand. It was like watching an arctic wind freeze her smile into ice.

As she called out the next student's name, she was compelled to take a handkerchief from her purse on the podium and wipe her hands. Good intentions aside, it was as unobtrusive as a cow walking across the stage. The audience roared with laughter.

This happened way back in the '70s, a lifetime ago. Yet to this day, envisioning that mortifying moment, the pain comes back with a rush as fresh as this morning's tabloid headline, "Timid Teen Attempts to Drown Teacher (Nationwide Hunt Underway)."

Over the years, I have realized that I am not alone. Some people today are (nearly) as pathetic as I. Fortunately for them there is a cure to the mushy mitt syndrome. Modern science gives us, the drum roll please, *antiperspirant.* If it works under your arms, it works on your hands. My hands still tend to perspire on an important occasion but when dressing for an event, no roll-on or spray for me. I use old-fashioned jar antiperspirant, and I make sure to massage it into my armpits with my bare palms.

But enough of the *don'ts.* Here are the *dos* for your handshake. Just as your physician listens to your heartbeat and peers into your eyes with that blinding little flashlight during your annual physical, here are the five points the handshake doctor would check you out on.

I open many of my communications seminars by having people shake hands with someone they don't know. Then, in the middle of the shake, I tell them to freeze.

Try it with a friend. Shake hands and, in the middle of the shake, become motionless. Have someone check you on the following five points.

1. Are you looking into each other's eyes? This is pretty basic. Yet, out of timidity or disinterest, many people catch themselves at the critical moment of contact, looking away. Here is a trick you can play to make sure your ocular nerve is focused in the right place: while your hands are pumping, make a mental note of your shakee's eye color.

2. Are the webs of your thumbs touching? What are the webs? Think of your hand as a big duck's foot. The web is the part between his toes, in this case your thumb and forefinger. Whenever you shake hands, you want to slide in with your hand until your webs press together in good fellowship. As you confidently glide your hand in, you'll be surprised at how many people grip and stop you before you get to their web. It sends out subliminal signals that they are afraid of intimacy.

3. Are you putting light pressure on their metacarpals? On their what? The metacarpals are the bones in the back of your hand. I said *light* pressure. That's why the bone crusher is called the bone *crusher*—those tiny bones are delicate crushable fossils. (And, the older you are, the more fossilized they become.)

4. Are your palms close enough together that you could hold a marble between your palm and your partner's? If your palms are pulling away from your partner's, you give the subliminal feeling that perhaps you have something to hide—you know, like those buzzers kids used to hide in their palms.

5. Are your palms 100 percent perpendicular to the floor? If you extend your hand knuckles up, palm down, you are saying, "I'm the boss! Anything I say goes. If I say jump, you ask me, 'How high?'" If you extend your hand palm up, you give the impression of a beggar, and the shaker feels he has to cross your palm with a tip.

With these five checkpoints, you will be a perfect shaker in no time.

Now you know the basics of the Five-Star Handshake, let's give it a little fine-tuning. How many pumps? Two should suffice lest your shakee thinks you're trying to draw water. Check your arm. Is it slightly bent? If it's too straight, it signals that you are fearful and are saying, "Stay away!" If it's too close, it could be anxiety provoking. They may fear you've pulled their hand in so tight they'll never get it back.

Are you leaning forward subliminally signaling, "I like you and would like to get closer to you." Or are you leaning back which in the language understood around the world says, "I'm trying to get as far away as is socially possible."

And, of course shake with one hand—unless you are giving your condolences: "I'm so deeply sorry your parakeet passed away." Let there be a momentary linger at the end of your handshake. If you are holding good strong eye contact and a bit of your dental work is showing in a sincere smile, it anchors the good fellowship that only a handshake has the power to make.

I've been trying to break the habit but, in the past several months, I've been judging everyone's handshake. More than once I've had to bite my tongue to resist saying to a new acquaintance, "Nice shake."

Clause #15: My Five-Star Handshake ♀♂

Whenever I shake hands, I will make sure (1) to maintain eye contact, (2) to have our webs touching, (3) to exert light pressure, and (4) to keep our palms marble-close and (5) perpendicular to the floor.

17 The Hugganary

You can't go anywhere these days without seeing people everywhere in A-frame stacks throwing pretentious air kisses. If someone lifts her arms, bends over at the waist, and comes at you with that "I'm soo cool because I'm going to give you zee French hug" look in her eyes, there's not much you can do to avoid it. But PMs try to make the moment mean something by making it, at least, an honest hug.

Several years ago, at a convention I learned the meaning of the more commonplace hugs.[26]

First is the A-Frame Hug. On the opening day of any convention, you spot everybody giving this one to folks they haven't seen since the last convention. Since they can't remember each other's name (and obviously haven't given them a thought since they went through the identical charade the year before), they cover it with a hug. Like pairs of cards with their tips balanced tent style, they are cheek to cheek but their bodies and feet are as far apart as humanly possible. The accompanying dialogue is always, verbatim, an effervescent, "Hello, how *are* you. It's so good to see you."

One step up is the A-Frame Patter's Hug. This is similar to the above with the addition of each patting the other's back. The added unspoken dialogue is, "It's been a long time. I really don't want to touch you though." The A-Frame Patter's Hug is also employed by friends of the opposite sex when they are genuinely happy to see each other but their respective spouses have accompanied them on this trip, so they don't dare upgrade to the more desirable Heart-to-Heart Hug.

Which, of course brings us to the Heart-to-Heart Hug which is, in my estimation, the first true hug. This is the uninhibited hug between two friends who really do like each other and are not uptight about it. Their full upper bodies are touching and their lower bodies are still separated, but by a smaller space. The underlying message is, "We're good friends. I really like you, but we're not having sex."

Women, unless one of them is too well endowed, often give each other the Heart-to-Heart Hug. Men do too, but their hugs last a fraction of the time that the female version does. One study on men's hugging showed that, even during these fleeting hugettes, "men often suffer marked psychological distress" lest one get the wrong idea.[27] I've often seen men, in a natural overflow of genuine sentiment, instinctively give each other a quick hug—and then look around furtively to see if anyone noticed.

Now we come to the famous *Big Bear Hug*, my favorite. It is known round the world and named after the celebrated grizzly bear.

Perhaps the Bear Hug is an intensely poignant concept to me because I once had a boyfriend who was a real Big Bear Hugger. In fact, not only did he hug a bear, he trained it to dance! Alfred (my boyfriend, not his real name, but he looked like one) kept Barney (the bear, his real name, and he definitely looked like one) in a big geodesic dome made of fencing material in his backyard in Iowa. However, he often traveled to New York with Barney to shoot movie scenes or commercials.

When Barney wasn't working, Alfred would charge admission for tourists to come watch him dance with Barney. They made a striking couple. Alfred was a slender, Aryan type with longish blonde hair. Alfred was tall, but Barney was taller (ten feet), heavier (weighing in at more than 1,000 pounds—before breakfast), and much hairier. That's a lot of bear to dance with. Just one of Barney's paws was larger than Alfred's head. It was upsetting to think of my relationship at the mercy of a bear. If Barney ever got upset with Alfred, he could smash his beautiful head with one swipe.

Alfred invited me out to Iowa to visit him for a few days and I learned the meaning of a "Bear Hug" the first time I saw them perform together. The show started and Alfred gave Barney one of a dozen commands he knows such as, "Turn around." Barney stared at Alfred blankly for a minute. Barney repeated, "Turn around, Barney." Then, to the delight of the crowd, Barney lifted one of his massive paws and started his turn in a clockwise direc-tion. When he had completed his pirouette and several other graceful (for a bear) moves, Alfred would go berserk with praise. He reached into his pockets which were stuffed with chicken giz-zards, necks, and legs and held them out. "Good Barney! Good Barney!" he boomed.

When Barney had greedily and happily devoured the prize, he clasped Alfred in a *big* hug. From that moment on, no one in the crowd would ever have the same image when they hear the words "Bear Hug" again. For the rest of their lives, 175 pounds of Alfred being surrounded almost 360 degrees by 1,175 pounds of Barney will flash before their eyes. And whenever they give someone a bear hug, it will be bigger and warmer and longer than ever.

But let me tell you about the last time I saw Alfred and Bar-ney do their thing. Everything had gone as planned. Barney had performed a dozen or so of his amazing feats. But this time, dur-ing the great hug, it must have dawned on Barney that Alfred couldn't move! And as long as Alfred couldn't move, he wouldn't be able to make him do any more silly things like ballerina turns. And maybe being top bear was better than getting chicken treats and wolfing them down for a crowd of tourists.

"Let go," I heard my dear Alfred say in a firm voice muffled by bear fur. I could hardly see my man inside of big Barney's grasp.

"Let go," he repeated, more muffled, but louder. Barney looked down at the tousled yellow head buried in his chest and then looked at the frightened spectators.

"Let go, Barney," Alfred said one more time. Barney responded by dropping some bear slobber on top of Alfred's head. Finally after what seemed like an eternity to me, he loosened his grip. Alfred, grinning from ear to ear, emerged from Barney's grasp, drenched but exhilarated. Alfred then blew into Barney's mouth (a sign of esteem and affection among bears) and more great globules of bear slobber slithered down on Alfred's head and down his back. Alfred seemed to love it.

I found myself becoming ill.

As a finale, Barney lay down on his back and put his paws in the air. Just kidding, Alfie.

Somehow I just couldn't bring myself to kiss Alfred after that. The end of a beautiful relationship. I guess it ended, as many relationships do, by seeing my man in the arms of another.

To this day, that scene of man and bear hugging each other was more sincere than any I've seen of two human beings hugging each other. Since then, I have tried to avoid superficially hugging someone unless I really feel it. But if I do, I hold them tight, if only for a second, like Barney held Alfie (and I try not to slobber on their head).

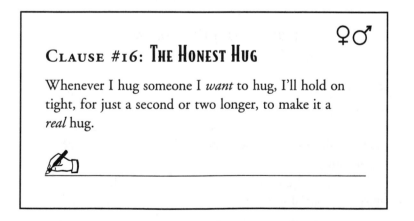

♀♂

Clause #16: The Honest Hug

Whenever I hug someone I *want* to hug, I'll hold on tight, for just a second or two longer, to make it a *real* hug.

18 The Secret of Confident Conversing

The secret of conversing comfortably and confidently can be reduced to three easy pieces. Dozens of studies have unveiled what makes a successful socializer, and they all came up with the same answer.

My all-time favorite study in this area is called "The Behavioral Assessment of Social Competence in Males."[28] That's a fancy name for "What makes a guy *cool*?" Even though this particular study involved men, the same rules apply to women.

What Separates Social *Winners* from Social *Losers*?

Researchers chose two groups of men to participate in the study. The first group was already successfully socializing. They were invited to many parties, were popular with women, and were well liked by all. These fellows dated a lot and were *winners* in the social scene.

The second group, alas, were not *winners*. In fact they were *losers* in the social scene. They wanted desperately to date, but they were either hesitant to ask a woman out or were continually getting turned down. Since the two groups of men were equally good-looking, researchers set about isolating what made one group of guys *winners*, and the second group *losers*. They put the men through a series of tests.

Would You Like to Dance? The first test took place at a social dance. The men were just told to ask someone to dance. The women (who were in on the study) were to respond by saying, "I'm not really much of a dancer."

> **Results:** Upon hearing this, the men who were successful with women did not interpret this answer as a rejection, but simply as a statement of fact. The successful men simply laughed and responded with variations of, "I'm not either. Why don't we just sit down and talk?"
>
> The less successful guys responded with a wide variety of "Oh," "Er," "Um, well," and the like, and then they gave up. In short, the "losers" interpreted the females' answers as rebuffs.

Hi, How Are You? In the second test, researchers taped conversations between attractive women and the *winners*, and between the same women and the *losers*. This time the women did not know it was a study. It was the gentlemen's assignment to chat with a woman for a while and eventually ask her for a date.

> **Results:** The difference between the *losers* (most of whom were turned down for the date) and the *winners* (who often got an affirmative answer) was this. The *winners* chatted, asked questions, and, immediately upon the woman's answer, offered their own experiences or views. Many of them then asked the woman another question to include her and keep the exchange going. In other words, they allowed very few pauses in the conversation. There was a continuous flow of energy. The conversations had a nice *melody* to them.

Now the *losers* had equally interesting and intelligent things to say. But, unfortunately, there were more awkward gaps in their conversations. They paused too long or hemmed and hawed before answering. The *musicality* of the exchange was off which made the women uncomfortable.

Researchers also timed the length of the men's answers to the questions the women asked. For instance, a woman asked, "Why did you move to Sacramento?" A *winner* would give a longer answer and then throw the ball back in her court. A *winner's* answer might sound something like this:

"Well, there were several reasons actually. One, I'd read a lot about Sacramento. I'd heard that it had a rich cultural life, especially theater. The weather is great, and the people very friendly. Also, I'm toying with the idea of studying veterinary medicine and California State University has a very strong reputation in that department. My sister moved here a few years ago, and she's been telling me nothing but good things about the city. How about you, were you born here or did you move here?"

A *loser's* answer might be, "Uh, well, because my sister was here and I wanted to go to California State University."

There was a third plus. The *winners* had high energy in their voices. They sounded truly interested in what they were saying, and the energy was catching.

The *losers* had many more pauses and shorter answers. When they did talk for thirty seconds or more, their voices were monotonous—not someone you'd want to listen to all evening.

To summarize, the big difference between the *winners* and the *losers*: First, the *winners* did not expect rejection. When they got turned down for the dance, they just let it roll off their backs, and they carried on the conversation. Expecting rejection is always a self-fulfilling prophesy.

Second, the *melody* of the conversation was smoother. In hearing a song for the first time, you listen to the melody before you decipher the lyrics. So it is in conversation. The *winners'* melodies were good because they reacted quickly to the women's questions and therefore eliminated awkward silences. When they did answer, rather than giving one-sentence answers, they talked longer. Their voices were energetic. They showed they were enjoying speaking with the women. They also showed they were interested by ending many of their responses with a question.

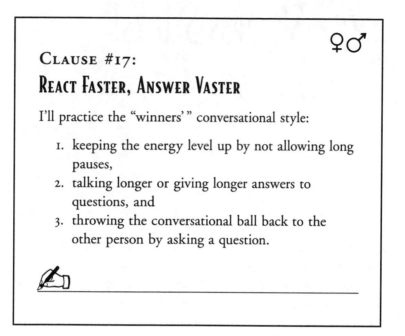

CLAUSE #17:

REACT FASTER, ANSWER VASTER

I'll practice the "winners'" conversational style:

1. keeping the energy level up by not allowing long pauses,
2. talking longer or giving longer answers to questions, and
3. throwing the conversational ball back to the other person by asking a question.

19 Shyness Stinks!

Not Only That, It Can Trash Your Life

OK, let's get real serious about shyness, because shyness is serious—real serious. Think back to when you were . . .

Age 4: Your mother called you *cute* when she ran into one of her friends in the grocery market and you hid behind her skirt. "She's shy," your mother would smilingly tell her friend.

Age 10: Your Dad was proud that, instead of going out and playing with the other kids, you preferred to stay home and play with your chemistry set. "Looks like he'll grow up to be a scientist," he bragged to his buddies. (Little did he know the other kids terrified you so much you preferred formulas to folks.)

Age 15: At the dinner table you tearfully tell Mom and Dad how shy you feel around the other kids, and you get the shakes whenever you have to talk to someone of the opposite sex. They look at each other and smile understandingly. "Oh, don't worry," they say. "It's just a passing phase. Everybody feels shy. You'll get over it." Your parents had no idea that they could be ruining your life by the way they treated your shyness.

First let's dispel that "you'll-get-over-it" inaccuracy. Approximately 30 to 48 percent of adult Americans suffer from shyness and consider it a lifelong hindrance.[29] Thirteen percent of these folks are in anguish owing to an acute case of the ailment. Shy people, at first meeting, are sometimes considered to be less intelligent, and they often consider themselves to be much less attractive than they really are. Because of their shyness, they never feel complete. They never attain a satisfactory *sense of self.*[30]

Wait, There Are More Bummers

Shy people have difficulty making friends, they date less, and if they do date, they're forever botching up the friendship or love affair. Shy people are less likely to find a partner and get married than those who suffer with other types of anxiety problems.[31] Shy women who do marry are less apt to blend raising a family with fulfilling outside interests or career. They are more apt to suffer loneliness and *empty-nest syndrome* when their kids grow up.

Furthermore, shy people are slower to get into a satisfactory career. And when they do, their careers are more unstable right on through midlife. They seldom find a job that utilizes their talents.[32]

Had enough? Well just one more round. Shy people suffer more from self-deprecatory thoughts,[33] inhibited behavior,[34] loneliness,[35] anxiety attacks,[36] and depression[37]—all documented in the studies numbered above.

Can I put it any stronger? Shyness sucks. Insecurity is the pits. It can trash your life. And the time to chuck it is *now.*

I'm no stranger to shyness. Right through college I suffered a severe case of schmooze-aphobia. I was much too timid to go to any social events alone. Early on, I had tried one where I stood in the same spot all evening rivaling the wallpaper for attention, and the wallpaper won.

In those days, I didn't have the benefit of role models. There were no movies where the socially challenged star miraculously overcame his or her dweebness and become popular. Kids are luckier now. There's a spate of teen movies with the evergreen Cinderella theme of mousie dweeb turning into prom queen and being courted by the *in* crowd. Or dorky dude winning the salami scarfing contest or some other unexpected awe-inspiring feat and thereby getting the girl and being loved by all.

So, If Schmooze-Aphobia Is a Disease, What's the Cure?

Only in the *misery likes company* department is it consolation to know that ten million American adults regularly suffer Social Anxiety Disorder.[38] If you're not one of those ill-fated ten million, you've still probably suffered an occasional attack of SAD—like when you have to give a speech or where you're expected to make sociable chit-chat at a party of strangers. The symptoms are familiar: racing heart, blushing, trembling, wishing you could say "Beam me up, Scottie" and be teleported to anywhere except where you are.

Without getting too deeply into a depressing discussion of dopamine, norepinephrine, and serotonin, suffice it to say that a chemical imbalance is often at the root of shyness or schmooze-aphobia. For severe chronic cases which inhibit one from functioning, psychiatrists can prescribe an antidepressant to increase the level of the neurotransmitter serotonin in the brain. But medication is not a satisfactory solution and it takes a lot more than a little yellow pill to make fear disappear, or a big orange one to make us more sociable, or a whopping red one to suppress the fear-'till-you-tear syndrome. Personality by prescription is a long

MORE MAGNETIC ATTRACTION!

Like learning to ski, think of the movements individually. Practice the fifteen clauses we've covered on all those people you ambush in the elevator or corner on the corner, and you'll soon be sliding through social occasions with the grace of a champion. Don't worry so much about the words at first. People Magnets know it's the melody that counts. They make their voices enthusiastic and keep their body language open and friendly. PMs make everyone they speak with feel special.

way off, if ever. There is no quick fix, but there are a few excellent home remedies for alleviating shyness. (They are the ones I used, and, happily, they worked.)

The first one is force yourself to talk to strangers. Do I hear, "But my parents told me when I was a kid never talk to strangers?"

You're no longer a kid. Avoid accosting strangers in dark alleys at night but talk to neighbors and other harmless looking street strollers in your neighborhood. But smile, open your mouth, and talk to people standing in line at the bank or waiting to get into a busy restaurant. A shyness clinic in California actually suggests getting on elevators just for the ride and snaring unsuspecting strangers for conversation.[39]

Another helpful hint is to get a dog, the funnier looking the better! I once invested in a Siamese cat who walked on a leash. This putting one foot after another after another after another while on a leash was such a rare feat for a cat that passersby made constant comments. I learned to laugh right through the hundredth time someone asked if my cat's name was Lassie.

People always have something to say about animals. I once was introduced to a short, rotund chap who works in the world-renowned Fulton Fish Market. I had always wanted to see the market, and I talked Marco into giving me a tour one morning. As he passed each booth, everyone gave him a big wave and a smile and said, "Hi Monkey Man" as though he were a celebrity. I asked Marco what they were talking about. He said he owned a pet monkey he usually carries on his shoulder, but, alas, the monkey had a hangover that morning. Obviously everyone was used to talking to Marco and his imbibing monkey.

Whether we walk with monkeys on our shoulders or cats on leashes, or we ride in elevators that go nowhere, the trick is to start talking with people everywhere. The more you do it, the easier it gets.

Learning how to be a natural-looking winner and glide smoothly through any social occasion like a hot knife through butter is not easy. You know all the right things to do, but putting them together, well that's another matter. The best way to proceed is to practice one or two clauses at a time. Perhaps just use Clause

#1, saying everything as though I were "In Your Shoes"; and giving everyone Clause #2 "Eye Messages" for a few days. When those become second nature, add numbers three and four, "The Expanded Thank-You" and "The Trifling Touch." And so on.

Getting these skills perfected is like learning to ski—incidentally one of the most humiliating experiences of my adult life. (If you have kids, teach them to ski *now* so they don't ever have to endure what I did.) There I was, a full grown and, if I must say, well-coordinated adult. I had bought new skis and a snazzy ski outfit and showed up for my first lesson. What could be so hard? The instructor gave me simple directions—bend your knees, keep your back straight, lean forward. Fine. Now look down the hill, lean into it, and keep your weight on the downhill ski. *Yeeoooooooooow!*

It was a long, long time before I was able to, without concentrating on all those separate activities, enjoy the pleasure of the fluid grace of my body speeding down the mountain, feel the cold wind on my cheeks, or even smile at the other skiers.

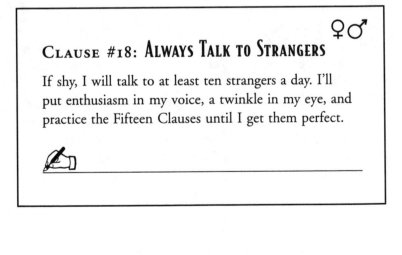

Clause #18: Always Talk to Strangers

If shy, I will talk to at least ten strangers a day. I'll put enthusiasm in my voice, a twinkle in my eye, and practice the Fifteen Clauses until I get them perfect.

20 Does This Confidence Make Cents?

Having the attitude that people will like you isn't good only for getting dates or socializing at parties. Confidence makes a lot of cents—which leads to dollars and, for one company, led to millions of dollars.

A University of Pennsylvania psychology professor gave a "personality survey" to reps at a major life-insurance agency. He asked, among many other questions, if, when they met someone, they believed the person would like them. The ones who answered, "Sure, they're going to like me, why not?" were called the *optimists* for the sake of the study. The rest were neutral or pessimistic about people liking them.

The optimists among them had no more training and no more experience. But in the months that followed, the optimists sold 37 percent more than the not-so-confident ones!

"Whew," thought top management of the insurance company. This professor Martin Seligman's study is very impressive. Because of it, they decided to go out on a limb. They took a chance and hired 100 wannabee reps who had actually *flunked* the standard industry exam but were real optimists on how much they thought they could sell.

More Magnetic Attraction!

The secret lies in the questions we ask ourselves. Your brain is a colossal computer. You ask it a question, it will find an answer. If it doesn't find an obvious one, it keeps searching and searching and searching—even if it has to go back to when you were two years old. Still no answer? Well, the brain is so determined, it will give you an answer, even if it's the *wrong* one. To have total control over their minds, PMs learn how to ask the right questions.

The company was being pretty optimistic by taking such a courageous move, but it paid off. These happy flunkers sold 10 percent more than the average guys and gals who had passed the exam.

So what happens when an optimist fails? Seligman said that when Gloomy Guses or Calamity Janes say or do the wrong thing, they tell themselves, "No wonder I botched that. I'm terrible at social (or business) situations." Or "I'm terrible when it comes to meeting women (men)."

Whereas Mr. Sunshine or Ms. Pollyanna says, "Whoops, I'll figure out precisely what I did wrong and resolve not to do that next time."

A similar dynamic shows up when things go well, Seligman explains. The crepe hanger says "It was just dumb luck—couldn't happen again." Whereas Dr. Pangloss pats himself on the back and says, "I knew my hard work would pay off!"

Suppose you make a mistake, you hit your head and say, "Why am I such a turkey?" Whiz, whiz, the disk starts spinning and voila! Your brain has found an answer. You're a turkey because you've always been a turkey, and you always will be a turkey. Now you feel miserable and the next move you make is a turkey move.

But, suppose you ask yourself a different question upon making a mistake. Your brain asks, "Hmm, what can I learn from this?" or, even better, "What can I do differently next time?" You'll be sure to find an answer and therefore probably not make the same mistake twice. The biggest winners in life and in love are people who have made each mistake once—only once. They also develop long arms so they can give themselves a daily pat on the back for the things they did well.

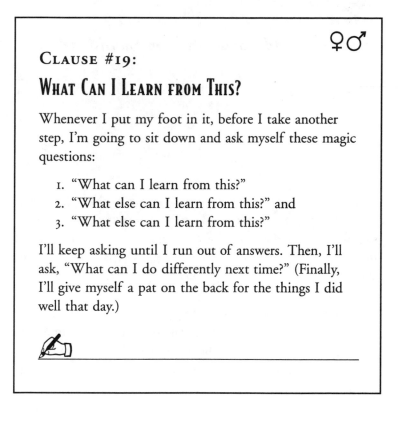

CLAUSE #19:

WHAT CAN I LEARN FROM THIS?

Whenever I put my foot in it, before I take another step, I'm going to sit down and ask myself these magic questions:

1. "What can I learn from this?"
2. "What else can I learn from this?" and
3. "What else can I learn from this?"

I'll keep asking until I run out of answers. Then, I'll ask, "What can I do differently next time?" (Finally, I'll give myself a pat on the back for the things I did well that day.)

21 Ah, Mystery of Life

And How Optimism Saved One!

One of the most pleasurable aspects of networking (and you'll get a great game plan for that later) is that sometimes a relationship which started as a professional one turns into a true friendship. And where there is true friendship, there is trust. This trust allows you to cross the line and say things off-the-record to your friend that you would never say publicly.

I'm proud to say that one of those friends is a highly esteemed cardiologist in New York who is on the staff of two important hospitals and a professor at one of the best medical schools. She lectures frequently and has been the cardiology consultant for several major publications. In other words, Carolyn (her name is changed) has credibility—big time. But Carolyn told me something across a dinner table that she could never say to a reporter or even a fellow cardiologist. Yet she is as convinced of it as she is of her own heartbeat.

She has no way of proving it, but she said, "If a patient truly believes he will survive—I mean truly truly believes it and isn't just trying to convince himself that he will get better—the chances are astronomically increased that he will." Here her voice faded off, and her eyes began to water as she leaned forward to tell me about one of her patients who had three heart attacks and was being treated for serious coronary artery disease. "When he was rolled down the corridor of the hospital for open-heart surgery, his family thought they'd never see him again. I didn't think they would either," Carolyn said.

"I visited him and clasped his hand, and he gave me a weak smile. He could hardly speak as he said, 'I'm not going to make it, am I Doc?' This man had complete trust in me. I had been treating him for six years, and he knew I always gave it to him straight. I'd yelled at him when he kept smoking and told him every cigarette was another nail in his coffin. Once I grabbed a cigarette out of his mouth in my waiting room right in front of other patients and told him if he was hell-bent on continuing to smoke I was going to drop him as a patient. Furthermore, if he wanted to kill himself, I told him, do it somewhere else!

"Anyway," Carolyn said, "he believed *anything* I said." She said she just stood over his bed looking into his eyes, not knowing what to say. She had never lied to him before. But this time it was different. She knew that if she told him what she really thought, that his family would never see him again.

He asked her again, "This is it, huh?" Carolyn is a deeply religious woman and would never tamper with the truth. Unless . . .

"Oh, come off it," she lied, "unless you've got some cigarettes hidden under that blanket, of course you're going to make it. You're going to be fine."

He believed it, and he was.

George died several years later, Carolyn told me. But she knows that big whopper she told him gave him the strength to pull through and it gave him and his family a few more years to share. Carolyn's beliefs don't permit her to say "God." But she laughed as she looked heavenward, and said she knows she'll be forgiven for the big whopper she told George.

There are even times when being an optimist can be a matter of life and death.

22 Pass the Pollyanna Please

If you already have kids, or someday plan to, one of the greatest gifts you can give your children is the gift of optimism, the faith that they can do whatever they want.

Carolyn was brought up in the days when the most accepted woman's aspiration was to go to college and bag a good husband. But her family didn't hesitate for a moment when she told them she wanted to grow up and be a heart doctor instead. My Texan friend Dale could trace his optimism back to his father's "I think I can, I think I can" choo-choo train optimism.

I have another super-achiever friend. When Benissa with her almond eyes, smooth milk chocolate complexion, and glistening black hair comes to work in the morning, she could easily be mistaken for one of the top models in the agency her firm represents. Instead, she followed a career in law and is senior partner at a prestigious Los Angeles firm specializing in the entertainment industry. No small accomplishment since entertainment law is extremely competitive and you've got to be a whole lot better than just "real good" to make senior partner. Add this to the fact that she's a woman, an African-American woman at that, and you've got one big winner here.

I was expressing my admiration to Benissa one day and she said, "Thanks, but I always expected to wind up doing this kind of work."

"But," I started to falter here, "being born in the fifties, before civil rights and all that, uh, you never thought you'd get this far, did you?"

"Sure," Benissa replied. "Dad always made me feel I could be anything I wanted to be. Remember when Neil Armstrong first stepped on the moon in 1969? I was ten-years-old then."

"Yes," I replied.

"Well, we lived in a really poor neighborhood in Brooklyn then. But Dad took the whole family on the subway into New York City to watch it on a big screen in Central Park. I was shorter than everyone else so Dad had me hoisted up sitting on his shoulders. I'll never forget that feeling. I was taller than anyone in the whole park. And when Neil Armstrong put his foot on the moon, that was me taking one giant leap for mankind.

"That night, when we got home, I told Dad I wanted to be the first woman on the moon. Instead of saying, 'Yeah, you and two million other kids. Off to bed now,' he smiled at me and we sat down to construct a serious game plan. 'First, you'll have to study astronomy and physics. Then you'll need some engineering background . . .'

"I went to bed happy that night knowing, if I wanted to be a female astronaut I could be. And that was always Dad's attitude," she told me. "Anything I wanted to be, I could be.

"As I got older, I decided against my extraterrestrial aspirations and decided I wanted to be a lawyer in the entertainment industry right here on terra firma. And, well, that's what I am— still dealing with stars, I guess. But a much less predictable kind," she added.

Benissa's father knew how important it was that his daughter believe she could do whatever she wanted. He had given her one of the most valuable gifts in the world, the gift of "You Can Do."

Clause #20:

Give the Gift of "You Can Do"

I will never tell any young people in my life—my brothers, sisters, cousins, my own children—that something is too difficult or they cannot accomplish a certain goal. In fact, I'll help them take the first step, even if it's in what I consider an impossible direction.

PART THREE

FRIENDS AND LOVERS

How to Find Them,
How to Keep Them

23 Why Have Friends?

Or Pollyanna Plummets into Pandora's Box

When I was a grinning little kid with too many teeth for my face, people passing me on the street would call out, "Well, hello there little Pollyanna." (She was the mythological muse who was always happy, always smiling.) Well, I got bigger—and finally, my face began to fit my teeth. But people kept calling me "Pollyanna" . . . because I kept smiling.

And *meaning* it! Each day, I had more to be happy about. By me, I had a charmed life. Just ask me why and I would have started blithering about how I somehow managed to flirt with all the *glamour* jobs. I became a model (after a nose job), a cruise director (cracking jokes for passengers who would laugh at *anything* because that's what you do on a cruise), a Broadway actress (well, I had one Broadway role), and a Pan Am flight attendant.

Was it really glamorous? Once while kneeling in the latrine, straining stinking water for a passenger's lost contact lens, someone asked me what I was searching for. I replied, "I'm looking for the glamour in my job." Whether the jobs were glamorous or not is definitely debatable, but I sure made them sound that way at parties!

Then, by the age Barbie dolls are expected to grow up, I'd somehow managed to convert my fun jobs into more *serious* endeavors. I tacked a few more university credits on to my degree, became a communications skills consultant, a corporate trainer, professional speaker, and author. My business life was brimming with blessings. Four books, a couple of cassette series, representation by the best speakers' bureaus, I had a lot to smile about. I was doing the work I loved and loving the work I was doing. I was still Pollyanna.

I won't say my friends called me that anymore, because now I didn't have a whole lot of friends. But, then, I didn't really take the time to invest in finding and nurturing friendships. After all, that would gobble up hours that I'd rather spend writing or planning a speech. I was a certified workaholic. Besides, I had one really good friend in my platonic male roommate (PMR) Phil. And I had a boyfriend too. His name was Giorgio.

Not only was my life happy, it was *secure*. All my ducks were in order. I had insurance on my house, my car, and my body which covered everything that could possibly go awry save a broken fingernail.

Yet the best insurance of all, I arrogantly told myself, was my own mind. I had confidence, thanks to my training in communications skills, that no matter what happened, I could talk my way into—or out of—anything I wanted.

Suddenly Last Summer

Then suddenly one summer as I was walking to a meeting—one that I had been looking forward to for some time—I felt a curious anvil-like weight on my heart, an alien joylessness. Why? I had just been chosen by the National Association of Female Executives as their Speaker of the Year and would do a cross-country tour of breakfast talks. This was the luncheon to meet the executive director and tour coordinator.

Why wasn't I my usual exhilarated self? Why had I misread the clock and arrived at the restaurant an hour late? Why, as I stared at the menu, was the thought of food repulsive? Why, as they chatted animatedly about the exciting itinerary, was I unable to concentrate? Why, when it came time to respond, was I uncharacteristically catatonic?

A puddle of perspiration trickled from my palms onto the napkin in my lap. Babbling fraudulent excuses, I bolted to the bathroom leaving the two women at my table looking at each other and wondering, I am sure, why the committee had ever chosen me. I grasped the sides of the sink to steady myself. Slowly I looked into the mirror. Staring back at me, I saw the ghoulish face of a frightened stranger with smeared makeup. *What was happening to me?*

Pollyanna Plummets into Pandora's Box

The next few weeks were a blur. I felt a poisonous black fog pressing down on me and squeezing out all my energy. With each breath I sucked in fear and exhaled any residual happiness. I lost twenty-five pounds and all my joy of life. By late August, I was a sorrowful 5'9", 110-pound scarecrow.

By September I realized I was not just having a series of *bad hair days*. I found myself, the author of *How to Talk to Anybody About Anything* afraid to talk to people; the author of *How to Make Anyone Fall in Love with You* unable to touch lipstick to my lips or powder to my nose. I let my machine answer the phone, and I only returned calls when absolutely necessary. The producers of my audiocassette series, ironically called *Conversation Confidence*, had just rolled out a national advertising campaign. And I, like a child in the protection of mother's skirts, wanted to hide behind the drapes, frightened of talking to the neighbors. My book *Talking the Winner's Way* had just come out, and I had to cancel the author's tour because my interviews would have sounded like "Talking the Loser's Way."

The smallest task became an unsurmountable challenge. I would stand frozen in the supermarket aisle facing a shelf of soups. Tomato? Vegetable? Chicken noodle? Beef Barley? Making a choice was an impossible task. Sometimes I would see a poverty stricken old woman squeezing each orange before deciding which to spend her few food coupons on. I would have traded my life for hers in a heartbeat. She was able to make a choice.

My friend Phil was confused and worried. To keep him from questioning further, I told him I was suffering a hormonal imbalance—one of those "woman things." (Men never question "female conditions.") But I knew, day by day, my mind was melting away.

Enter Giorgio, a ship's captain by profession, and, as I gratefully discovered, a caregiver by nature. Giorgio took me to my little weekend cabin and stayed with me around the clock. He cooked for me, cared for me, and tried the impossible—to comfort me during my ever-worsening nightmare.

Sometimes I truly believed it was a nightmare, and if I screamed loudly enough, I would wake up. But woefully, there was no awakening from the mysterious malady.

September was just the beginning of the indescribable and inexplicable horror that lasted three months, fifteen days, and seven hours. By October, checking E-mail or balancing my checkbook and paying bills became mind boggling tasks. Numbers danced on the page to mock me. When I wrote checks, I added wrong, transposed numbers, and made puzzling mistakes. (The garbage collectors must have smiled as they returned my check written for $4,465.00 instead of $44.65.) The terrifying words "tear on perforation and fold" or "write account number on your check" were printed on bills just to taunt me. Did they have no mercy for the helpless?

The Bottom of the Pit

In November, the anguish became too intense to bear. I frightened Giorgio when I told him I wanted relief at any cost. When he walked me to a nearby state park, he held my hand securely because I told him every passing car looked to me like a machine, which, if I timed my lunge just right, could end my suffering. In the park, I looked up at the cliffs and mentally measured each, calculating if it was high enough and the landing hard enough to assure instant relief. I knew these were the contorted thoughts of a mind that was, as the doctor told me, *temporarily* depressed. But when even the next five minutes seemed like an eternity, I couldn't keep my thoughts out of this alien territory.

December came, and temperatures plummeted below zero. Now I was reduced to writhing and curling like a caterpillar with a pin through its belly on the couch. Because I had been unable to open the bills, the utility company suspended service. And, for once, Giorgio couldn't help. Because English was not his mother tongue, it was difficult for him to call and explain that it was just an oversight, and that the check was forthcoming.

Years before, when I was a flight attendant, I once asked the instructor of a crash-training course, "How long should we stay with a downed plane to help passengers?" The reply was, "Until the fire gets too hot, or the water gets too high."

Well, now the fire was too hot, and the water was too high, to keep up a front to the world that everything was OK. In as unfaltering voice as I could muster, I called Phil and told him the truth—that I was suffering what the doctors called a "severe depression." Could Phil assist me by opening my mail, paying the bills on my account, and sending the checks to my country home so Giorgio could steady my hand as I signed?

As though I'd told Phil I had a toothache and asked for an aspirin, my friend readily replied, "Of course, Leil." Then, he tried to comfort me by putting me in elite company. He said, "Many great writers have experienced a severe depression—Albert Camus, William Styron, Virginia Woolf, Jack London, Ernest Hemingway."

I appreciated his effort but had no ego left to massage. Besides, he neglected to mention that the last three of these fallen artists put an end to their anguish by their own hand.

In mid-December, I was able to calm the howling tempest in my brain just long enough to have the first thought in months that was not completely tormented and self-obsessed. For a glimmering moment, I was filled with gratitude to Phil and Giorgio, and I was overcome by the incredible power of friendship.

In the following weeks, I started having ephemeral flashes of rational thought. I devoted those moments to thinking of my two dear friends and how each was giving 100 percent of his capability. Each had made a very different contribution. Giorgio was a loving and patient caregiver but couldn't tell a piece of junk mail from an IRS audit notice, or speak English to a utility company. Phil was a brilliant writer and a virtuoso of organization, but couldn't take care of a cat, unless he'd programmed it into his computer.

I now truly believe that friends are God's way of taking care of us. Without one, the life I'd carefully constructed would have shattered; without the other, I might not even have a life.

So What's This Got to Do with How to Be a People Magnet?

Everything. Until this bout with depression, my doctrine was "we are our own best friend." Like so many motivational speakers, I preached this from my podium. I proclaimed that, no matter what adversity should come our way, we would always have our own mind and spirit to sustain us.

Now I know that there is no dungeon darker than the mind, and even your own spirit can betray you. You can become your own worst enemy. When that happens, you need friends and loved ones to intervene and shield you from the vicious and well-armed adversary who knows every back alley of your brain.

I had purchased many kinds of insurance policies. However, I never paid premiums on the most important one. This is the one you can't buy, but you still must pay for. The currency is not money. You pay in your time, your personality, and your love. It's the insurance of having loyal friends and true love. It's the only one that will save you when you really need it.

Pandora's Box Suddenly Snaps Shut

As the Christmas holidays and the New Year approached, flickering flashes of momentary relief began to give me hope. Had my mind finally balanced the scale against a lifetime of being overly energetic and effervescent? The anguish of those three months seemed an expensive price, but perhaps it had to be paid. Or was it simply that the medicine was starting to work?

In those fleeting seconds, I was able to function—make a phone call, sign a few checks. But the moments were all too brief, and I would again be metamorphisized into the agonized caterpillar.

December 30: Curled on the couch in the fetal position which had now become my permanent pose, I struggled to lift my leaden head to look at the clock. As I watched, as I had so often before, the second hand crept with excruciating sluggishness from 4:04 P.M. to 4:05, something different was happening. I felt a refreshing breeze on my back for the first time in months. Was the poisonous fog starting to swirl upward and outward and suck the torment out of my brain. *Could it be?* Was I really seeing a brilliant streak of the day's waning sunlight through the window for the first time since September?

At 4:05 P.M., the writhing caterpillar uncurled and shed its skin. I felt like a butterfly escaping its cocoon. I stood up tall, threw my shoulders back, and my arms floated up in the air. Dare I think I was free?

Dazed, I turned momentarily to look behind me down at the couch that had been my hideous home for so long. I saw a depression in the shape of my knees and head—like the contour of Mother's corpse in the mattress at the Bates Motel in *Psycho.*

That's what my experience is to me now. A scary movie that's over. Why my brain decided to take a four-month vacation, I'll never know. One doctor suggested that a workaholic's life not balanced with friends and loved ones leaves an emptiness that leads to a crash. Another explained a life of being manic can induce a depressive period. He said it's what they used to call a "nervous breakdown" and now they have a fancier word, "unipolar," which simply means a once-in-a-lifetime humongous depression. They both humbly agreed that modern medicine does not have the answers. All I know is that my brain, if it was going to take a vacation, could have chosen a better place to spend it than in hell!

May I pause for a "public service announcement" which, I pray, never becomes relevant for you? But if it does (it has been estimated that one in ten Americans will suffer from depression) and your mind should ever plunge into that abyss, please don't let pride shield you, as it did me, from immediately seeking the help you need. Tell your doctor when you detect the first dark shadow. And keep the faith. You *will* come back. And, I promise, when you do, you will see life with more serenity and joy than you ever imagined possible. And your spirit, having been contorted and twisted into unfathomable shapes, will possess even more capacity and desire to love.

December 31: I spent a glorious New Year's Eve with Giorgio, Phil, and his girlfriend, Colleen. "Pollyanna" had the happiest New Year ever. And her New Year's resolution? Make more friends, and help others to do the same.

Thus this book, *How to Be a People Magnet.*

24 Friendship's First Commandment

Thou Must Have Something to Give in Order to Receive

You've heard the phrase "nothing in life is free," or "there is no such thing as a free lunch." Is it sad but true? I don't think so. It's just true but true. No, I'm not a cynic. And yes I believe deeply in the power of love. Let me explain.

My friends Phil and Giorgio gave everything of themselves, 100 percent selflessly during the days when I thought there would be no tomorrows. Did they care for me night and day for what they thought they were going to receive in return? No, they did it because they were my true friends.

But let's carry this back to its logical inception.

Question: Why were they my true friends?
Simple answer: Because they liked me.

Now let's go another step back.

Question: Why did they like me?
Here the answer is not so simple. Perhaps they liked my way of thinking, or the knowledge I shared with them, or the laughs we had together, or the things I did for them, also selflessly. Whatever the reason, true friends are people who have a *history* together.

They are people who have received something from each other. That something can be anything.

Perhaps the something is new knowledge. Anaïs Nin wrote, "Each friend represents a world in us, a world possibly not born until they arrive, and it is only by this meeting that a new world is born."

Or maybe it is self-knowledge. Thus George Herbert's expression, "The best mirror is an old friend."

Or helping you grow. Henry Ford maintained, "My best friend is the one who brings out the best in me."

Or just making your days more pleasant. John Lubbock said, "A friend is like a sunny day spreading brightness all around." (And John should know all about things like sun 'n' stuff because he was an English astronomer.)

Or helping you make sense of your own thoughts. "A friend is one to whom one may pour out all the contents of one's heart, chaff and grain together, knowing that the gentlest of hands will take and sift it, keep what is worth keeping and with a breath of kindness blow the rest away," says an Arabian proverb.

Or someone who won't judge you. Mother Teresa believed "If you judge people, you have no time to love them."

Or maybe the gift they give you is comfortable silence, the contentment to be with them when you don't feel like talking. "When the silences are no longer awkward, you know you are around friends" is a proverb.

Maybe the gift your friend gives involves some self-sacrifice. "A friend is someone who is there for you when he'd rather be anywhere else."

Or keeps you on track with your dreams when you falter, or believes in you when you've ceased to believe in yourself. "A friend is someone who knows the song in your heart and can sing it back to you when you have forgotten the words."

Whatever the reason for your being friends, you have given them something of value, and they have done the same. To have a good friend, you have to be one. Kahlil Gibran wrote, "Friendship is always a sweet responsibility, never an opportunity."

You Don't Make Friends, You *Earn* Them

If we were chiseling friendship truths on a tablet, the first commandment would be: Thou Must Have Something to Give in Order to Receive.

Does that sound dangerously like barter, tit for tat? It is, in a way. If I had not given selflessly of myself to my two friends, they might not have done the same for me. Had I been humorless, stupid, and selfish—in other words if I had no "gifts" to give them, they would not have been inspired to give theirs to me. Had they been the same, I would not have been inspired to give mine to them.

Many a true and lifelong friendship or love relationship develops just because of someone's specific gift. I met Phil at a writing seminar "back in DOS days," as he says. At the time I was trying to make sense of then-new words like COBOL, PASCAL, FORTRAN, and other "insider" words that many computer techies tried to trick us with. They said we had to understand all that just to boot up our machines. Anyway, Phil and I had a brief conversation—or I should say he listened patiently to my whining monologue of computer woes.

"Hmm, I might be able to help you with that."

Hallelujah! It was like the skies opening and the computer god saying, "You have been saved." Phil came over the next afternoon and got my computer up and humming happily in just a few hours. Naturally, out of gratitude, I asked him to stay for dinner and a friendship developed.

♡MORE MAGNETIC ATTRACTION!

People Magnets know if they want dynamic friends drawn to them, they *must* keep growing. When people become too predictable, boredom sets in and the relationship suffers.

What did I have in return? No talent as valuable as his to share, but I did have some empty space in my loft which I was thrilled to have a fellow writer and computer genius rent, thus he became my Platonic Male Roommate (PMR).

And Yes, You Earn Lovers Too

Did a great hue and cry go up when I said that although a true love relationship is selfless, caring, and altruistic, you have to "bring something to the table" to first earn that love? You can earn it with your God-given gifts or ones that you develop.

A vast body of research called the *equity* theory (which I covered much more thoroughly in my book, *How to Make Anyone Fall in Love with You*) has shown beyond reasonable doubt that people make decisions about a potential love partner with all the reckoning that they would in buying a house or a horse.[40]

What is the *legal tender* that counts in love? Equity theorists reduced it to six: looks, money, prestige, intelligence, personality, and character.[41] They call it "the currency which buys a good partner."

Breaking the qualities and *assets* down into these six categories, of course, has its fallacies. People define words differently. Additionally this doesn't take into consideration other factors like religion, age, how many children they want, how their family feels about the partner, and what their *definition* of a relationship is.

That aside (and that's a pretty hefty *aside*), what I did find fascinating, was the accuracy with which equity theory was able to predict whether two people would be happy together based on what they bring to the table. I present this only as an example of how some researchers are so convinced of the tit for tat in relationships, that they have broken it down into calculable numbers. This, of course, supports our thesis that the way to draw more friends and lovers to you is to have more gifts to share. Or as equity theorists would say, more currency.

Clause #21: Growing My Gifts

To draw more friends and lovers to me (and/or be a better friend and lover to those I have), I will consciously grow my gifts in all areas—appearance, knowledge, finances, personality, prestige, and, most importantly, character.

25 Ways to Say "I Love You" to a Friend

Many women today value their friendships with other women as much as they do their relationships with men, maybe more. Just ask Baby, Scary, Posh, Sporty, and Ginger. ("Who?" do I hear fellow baby boomers ask?) They were called the Spice Girls and they reflected today's feeling about women's friendships in their song "Wannabe." You've heard it even if you couldn't understand the lyrics: "If you wanna be my lover, you gotta get with my friends. Make it last forever, friendship never ends."

Well, sister baby boomer, we should take pride that we were the first to acknowledge that a woman could have deep feelings for a woman, or that a man could have deep feelings for a man, with nothing sexual between them. This was an awareness we passed on to our own Babys (or Scarys, Poshs, Sportys, or Gingers). In their parents' day, it wasn't that way. A woman wouldn't think twice about changing plans made with a female friend, even at the last minute, if a date with a male came along.

26 Plan Private Pleasures for Precious People

One Saturday evening when I was a senior in high school, my best friend Stella and I had planned to go to the movies. She borrowed her brother's car so we could make an evening of it and drive to Chinatown for dinner afterward.

On that Saturday afternoon, the phone rang. I assumed it was Stella calling to set the time she would come by in her brother Spencer's snazzy little Nash Rambler. (Incidentally, Spencer was a pretty snazzy rambler himself. I'd had a secret crush on him ever since I saw him at Stella's house two years earlier. But it was unrequited infatuation. Spencer already had a steady main squeeze.)

When I picked up the phone, instead of Stella, I heard the nasal voice of Freddy, a freckle-faced fellow with skunk breath whom I had met at a party a few weeks earlier. Unfortunately Freddy was, as we used to say in those days, "strictly from Dullsville, USA."

My mother happened to be walking by my room as I said to him, "Oh, gosh, Freddie, you know how I would love that. Going to the party with you would be super." (In those days, we were taught to carefully lie to save a man's ego.) My mother was beaming at me from the doorway. "But," I continued, "I have plans to go to the movies with my girlfriend tonight." I could imagine his flabbergasted freckles paling in incredulity that I was turning him down, a bonafide male, for an engagement with a *girlfriend*. After I hung up, I looked at my mother and sensed something was terribly wrong. She reminded me of a duck whose feathers are unruffled on the surface, but underneath the feet are paddling frantically.

Mama cleared her throat and asked, "Leilie, dear, did I just hear you turn down a date to go to a party with a *boy* just because you told Stella you'd go to the movies with her tonight?"

"Yes, Mama, that was Freddie and going out with him would be duller than watching paint dry. I like Stella a hundred times more than I like him."

"Nevertheless, dear," she chided, trying to suppress her exasperation, "you can see Stella anytime and Freddie is a *date*."

"Mama, his breath is so bad I could smell it over the phone."

My mother gave me a strange look, probably questioning for a fleeting moment, her daughter's sexual orientation. Her retort was, "Well, you'll never meet any boys in a movie. You know I've always said, 'Go out with the creep, look over the crop.'" With that piece of misguided wisdom, Mama strode out of my room. (Not her finest moment.)

The next call was from Stella. I told her what happened, and we both got a big laugh out of it. I could tell that underneath her laughter was a tone of gratitude. Our feelings for each other were seldom verbalized but always understood. She planned to pick me up at seven.

I mentioned Stella's brother—tall, handsome, considerate, strong, gentle, intelligent, witty, and, I discovered, recently broken up with his previous girlfriend. Guess who rang my doorbell at seven? You're right. (God is good.)

Spencer took my arm to help me down my front steps to his car where Stella was waiting like a Cheshire cat.

I had never told Stella about my crush on her brother. But, looking back at it, of course she knew. Part of being a good friend is knowing things about your friends that they don't want to say and respecting that boundary.

The three of us had a great time. But the highlight for me was after the movie when we went to a Chinese restaurant. Spencer looked at me and said, "It really was great of you to turn down the date with that Adonis Stella told me about."

"That what?" I asked choking on my chow mein.

"Yeah, Stella told me about the football player who wanted to take you to the big Phi Sigma Kappa bash tonight."

"But . . . ," I started to protest.

"Oooooh," squealed Stella, "just try one of these dumplings," she said as she squished a whole fried pork dumpling dipped in hot pepper sauce into my mouth, temporarily incapacitating my tongue. "They are dee-lish!"

"No, really, I admire your loyalty to my sister," he said as I tried to extinguish the fire in my mouth.

I looked at him and tried to smile with my mouth full of ice cubes. When he smiled back, suddenly in my head, I heard a twelve-piece orchestra striking up the chords to "Falling in Love Again."

If Stella had told me she was going to bring her brother, I would have been thrilled. But not anywhere near the degree I was when it turned out to be a carefully conceived surprise just for me.

Had I listened more carefully to the orchestra playing in my head, I would have heard the strains of another song, one dedicated to Stella called, "That's What Friends Are For."

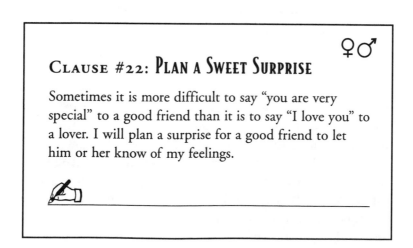

Clause #22: Plan a Sweet Surprise

Sometimes it is more difficult to say "you are very special" to a good friend than it is to say "I love you" to a lover. I will plan a surprise for a good friend to let him or her know of my feelings.

27 I Love Ya Man, and All That Jazz

Fellas, I'm just talking to you now. Suppose you have a good buddy, a real pal. You'd stick together through thick or thin, lose or win. You'd rush to the ramparts with a broken beer bottle to help him. You love the guy. And, in all these years, you've never said a word about how you feel. Do you have a friend like that? And did you ever tell that amigo, that compadre of yours, how much you value your friendship?

If you answered, "yes," congratulations. You are a rare and fine specimen of manhood indeed. If you answered "no," no problem. You've answered the way 95 percent of all guys do. In addition, you probably thought, "Don't need to say it. He knows."

And, yes, you're right, he probably does. And you can leave it at that. The spill-your-guts-at-the-drop-of-a-beer-bottle so called men's movement of the 1980s has pretty much blown over, and, confused as they are, nearly every man is still pretty happy just being a guy and acting in all the guy ways.

So why should I bring up the subject of letting a friend know how much he means to you? Well, because you bought this book called *How to Be a People Magnet*. And I assume you knew it meant not just love between a man and a woman. So, even though your buddy knows how you feel about him, maybe you should give him a shot before he's floatin' around flipped over and glassy-eyed in the goldfish bowl.

This following clause enriches your friendship with your buddy. He probably won't tell you, but when you let him know how much he means to you, he will appreciate it big time. However you want, do it at the proper time and in the proper way. You know the old saying, "There is a time and a place for everything." Well, they've even done studies on where and when one real man can tell another real man of his affection and still retain full butch status.

How about you? Put a tick mark by the place or places where you think the ol' boy would enjoy hearing how important he is to you.

_____ In a public place

_____ In private, where no one can hear

_____ At a sporting event

_____ While watching TV together

_____ At a wedding or funeral

♡ MORE MAGNETIC ATTRACTION!

Gentlemen, if you wish to inform another gentleman of your esteem and affection and not lose one ounce of testosterone, here's how: choose a public place, preferably an emotionally charged one like a wedding, funeral, or graduation. You're safe letting it all hang out—for about three seconds. Then pull back. You'll strengthen the bond and still remain stud-duck in the pond.

_____ Just walking along the street

_____ In the showers at the gym

Pass the envelope please. Well, "the showers at the gym" is definitely out if you want to keep your rep as a skirt chaser. The place men felt most comfortable giving or receiving a hug or hearing, "I love you, man" was in public.[42] Researchers determined the reason for this is that public displays of affection between romantic partners is less appropriate in public than in private. So, counterintuitively, two males hugging in public seems the antithesis of romance.

The best place, a study called "The Male to Male Embrace: Breaking the Touch Taboo in a Men's Therapy Group" decreed, is a wedding, funeral, graduation, or some other emotionally charged event.[43] That's when the sentiment sometimes wells up in real macho types who would never dream of saying anything warm and fuzzy to their good ol' buddyroo. It just sort of spills over at one of those events where it's appropriate to cry. (Well, a suppressed tear or two as the women are wringing out their handkerchiefs.)

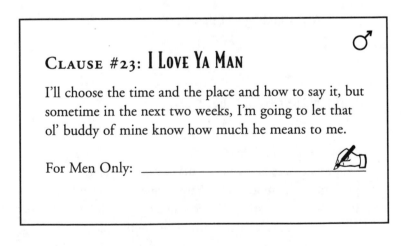

CLAUSE #23: I LOVE YA MAN

I'll choose the time and the place and how to say it, but sometime in the next two weeks, I'm going to let that ol' buddy of mine know how much he means to me.

For Men Only: _____

28 Actions Speak Louder than Words

Just Ask Any Guy

The next time you are at a sporting event, let your eyes scan the crowd. Lots of men. Everywhere men. Busloads of men.

Two males at a baseball game—without taking their eyes off the field for hours or saying anything other than "Kill the ump" or "Gimme me a coke 'n' a hotdog. What? Six fifty?"—are having as deep communication as any two women sharing their most intimate secrets.

They're on the same wavelength, just like two guys riding the crest of the same breaker on their surfboards, or two men's hands on the same bent rod trying to tug a massive fish out of the ocean. That's intimate communication, guy style. I once saw a film of six skydivers, holding hands, men would never do that except ten thousand feet up in a free fall. It was like their souls were one, and they were all entering the pearly gates together. (Could have happened!) Yeah, guys bond through stuff like that.

Men, here's a clause which will help you strengthen your friendships with other men, macho style. Women, don't feel left out. You, too, can use it to augment your cross-sex friendships, or even a potential love relationship. Whatever your motives, it helps the user to bond, big time, with the boys.

First write the name of a dude you'd like to schmooze. Then, under his name list some activities you know he enjoys. Fly fishing? Karate? Racquetball? Backpacking? Scuba Diving? Whitewater rafting? Mumblety-peg?

Name of a male friend _____

Some of his favorite activities:

I. _____

2. _____

3. _____

4. _____

5. _____

Now go over the list of activities and see which you have done, or could bluff your way through well enough to keep your friend's co-enthusiasts moaning, "Who brought that newby-nerd into our big deal interest?"

Now, where this gets hot—no, explosive—is when a woman puts together this little package for a male friend. If there's any romance potential there, this bonding match can light a stick of dynamite between them. (Women, when was the last time you called a man up and told him you had tickets to a baseball game?)

Once this technique worked, quite by accident. I have a friend Tara who is an editor in a publishing house. She is now married to the president of the company, a distinguished gentleman named Marvin. When she met him, he was as eligible and sought after as Bill Gates was at Microsoft in his single days. The female editors didn't go so far as to wear "Marry Me Marv" T-shirts like the "Marry Me Bill" T-shirts wannabee Mrs. Gateses did at Microsoft. However, other female employees shamelessly let the first button on their blouses come unbuttoned, or a shoe dangle while speaking with him. Nevertheless, publishing-mogul Marvin was strictly business all the way.

One Thanksgiving, Tara's brother who was a zealous hockey fan came to visit her. He coaxed, cajoled, and finally convinced poor Tara who didn't give a flying puck about hockey to accompany him to a big NHL game.

Unfortunately for Tara's brother, a business emergency cut his stay short. So there sat Tara with two expensive tickets for the best seats in the house. Tara had only one other slight connection with hockey in her life. She remotely remembered having seen photos of hockey players in Marvin's office. She wouldn't have noticed, but she remembered wondering what they were doing with those funny looking sticks.

Quite correctly, she sent an E-mail to Marvin telling how her brother couldn't use the tickets and if Marvin or any of his friends would like to go, please accept the tickets.

In less than sixty seconds after she clicked the send button on her computer, Marvin was on the threshold of her cubicle to say thank you. Now, gentlemen, a 5'10" gorgeous redhead gives you two tickets to a sold-out game you've been dying to go to—who are you going to take?

"Tara, do you enjoy hockey?" he asked.

Now women, suppose you despise the sport but fancy the man. Don't you think you could justify just one eensy-teensy little lie?

Tara said, "I do!"

A man bonds not only to another man by doing things they enjoy together, a man bonds to a woman by doing things he enjoys together. Less than a year later Tara was answering "I do" to another of Marvin's questions.

It came out (after their marriage) that Marvin had always admired Tara's excellent work, not to mention—because he was too reserved—her beauty. Tara had always respected Marvin's wisdom and administrative abilities, not to mention—because she was too reserved—the fact he was a hunk. Sometimes all it takes is a little puck to bring people together.

Women, let me issue a word of warning if you simply wanted to strengthen a friendship with a man and not have him get the wrong idea. When I told this story to a female friend of mine, she said he'd probably assume the woman was making a pass at him. I argued that I thought he'd just take it at face value because, when it comes to men, they miss so many things.

But, rather than argue with nothing to substantiate my claim, I did a little research. She was right. If an action could be taken either sexually or nonsexually, men will probably go for the former.

In a study called "Can Men and Women Differentiate Between Friendly and Sexually Interested Behavior?", approximately eighty men and eighty women were shown films of a male and a female acting in either a friendly or sexually interested fashion.[44] Men read a lot more sexiness into all the vignettes than the women. It was probably wishful thinking, so be careful.

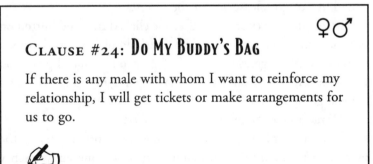

CLAUSE #24: **Do My Buddy's Bag**

If there is any male with whom I want to reinforce my relationship, I will get tickets or make arrangements for us to go.

29 The Power of Gifts

*Or a Great Way to Get Rid of Junk
You Don't Want!*

Are you a squirrel or a caterpillar? Some people are like squirrels who hoard and amass everything. They seem constitutionally incapable of throwing anything away. (Unfortunately, that's me.) Others are like caterpillars who are constantly shedding their skins and moving around in a new one. Like the date stamped on the top of a milk carton, everything in their life has a thirty-day expiration. (That's Phil, my PMR.)

It's almost a ritual now. Every Tuesday and Thursday evening, together, we lug the garbage down from our three-flight walk-up to the street for pickup. Inevitably, a few hours later, I'll have trouble sleeping thinking about how I'll miss one whatchamacallit or another that we've just junked. I then tiptoe to the door of his room to assure I hear the rhythmical regular breathing of deep sleep. That's my cue to sneak down in the dead of night and rescue that thingamabob.

Once, we had struggled together for almost an hour to carry a huge armchair down to the street. Long after he had gone to bed in exhaustion, I was still rearranging the furniture in my room. As I adjusted and readjusted the bed, the couch, and a few tables, I had one empty corner—the corner that was *perfect* for the just-discarded armchair!

I raced to the window. Whew, it was still there. Hmm, now a dilemma. Should I awaken Phil and with great embarrassment, ask him to help me lug it up again? No, the humiliation would have been too great, and, besides, he'd never let me forget it. Instead, I went down the street and found the panhandler who frequented our corner. "The Bum," by his own designation, and I were old friends by now. We had a deal. He wouldn't hold his hat out as I passed, especially if I was walking with friends, and in return, I would cross his palm with a little weekly payoff.

This time, I had bigger rewards for "The Bum." I asked him if he would like to earn ten dollars by helping me carry something? He smiled from ear to ear—until I pointed to the big armchair. His dismayed expression made me reconsider my weekly donation. Nevertheless we got the chair upstairs, and the next day Phil, spotting the chair as he passed my room, respectfully didn't say a word.

For some time now, Phil had been suggesting a let-go-of-clutter system he'd been using for years. It was, quite simply, throwing out three things a day. I tried it. The first day it was an old lamp, a tape recorder that I'd been planning to have fixed for three years, and an earring that I'd lost the mate to two years before. The second day it was a ripped sheet I knew I'd never sew, an old WordStar computer book, and three left gloves whose mates had been lost.

I held to this schedule for a week, and it was working well. I began to appreciate this shedding of effluvia. So, can you imagine my dismay when Phil's then-girlfriend, Felicia, a flight attendant, started bringing me little presents from places she traveled to—*tchotchkes* she called them. Tchotchkes (pronounced chachkeys) are little anythings. She brought me an carved ivory cigarette holder from Alaska (I don't smoke), Droste chocolate from Holland (I don't need the calories), and a coffee mug from Brazil (I prefer cups). Thanks to Felicia, I now have a box overflowing with ashtrays from around the world, little liquors from the plane, exotic shampoos and hand lotions from hotels' amenities trays, and three miniature Eiffel towers and one leaning tower of Pisa— junk, all junk. All things that I will gratefully shed, three by three.

But here's the rub. I adored Felicia for her thoughtfulness. Her little nothing gifts were a lovely tribute, much nicer than a postcard on which the sender has written in invisible ink between the lines, "Ha ha, look where I am now and you are not."

I was genuinely sorry when she and Phil broke up. Felicia and her tchotchkes had made me think about the concept of gift giving which is, by comparison, conspicuously absent in our culture.

Gift giving is expected between any two parties doing business in practically every other European or Asian nation. Each has unspoken rules on when and how you give the gift. Before doing business abroad, bone up on the particulars. Do you present your gift when you first meet, or at the end of the meeting? In private, or when others are around? Wrapped or unwrapped? Open it when you receive it or open it later? The list goes on. The important thing is not the value of the gift, but the fact that it is a gift.

Pick up little gifts not only while you're traveling, but while at home too. It shows you revere the receiver.

Incidentally, be aware of some gift-giving dos and taboos around the world. You are probably not sending the message you want if you give liquor to Arabs or chrysanthemums to Germans. And giving a clock to the Chinese or knives to Americans sort of says, "Drop dead!"

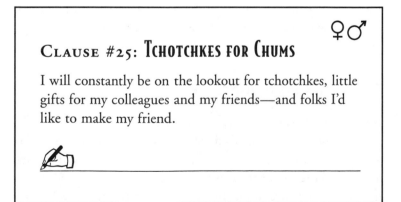

♀♂

Clause #25: Tchotchkes for Chums

I will constantly be on the lookout for tchotchkes, little gifts for my colleagues and my friends—and folks I'd like to make my friend.

30 Standing Up for Your Friends

A girl named Priscilla—my eyes narrow even now as I write her name—was *the* most popular girl in my school. All the girls wanted to bask in the shadow of this self-appointed princess. They tried to walk like her, talk like her, and dress like her. Monday, if Priscilla wore a sequined sweater to school, on Tuesday, you'd be blinded by the swarm of sequined sweaters in the classrooms. One Friday morning, she came to school with a dime instead of a penny in her loafers. By 10 A.M. Friday morning, not a pair of *penny* loafers was walking the halls. It was dimes everywhere.

The Green-Eyed Monster in My Closet

Lunchtime was cafeteria style with picnic tables and supposedly open seating. Open as a nailed coffin! Only Priscilla and her cool clique sat at the table by the window. Every day, as Priscilla approached the end of the cafeteria line, several of her cool clique groupies would race ahead to Prissy's table to scramble for the bench position next to where they predicted the Princess would place her most-prized posterior.

Was this being liked? I thought so then.[45] But no, this was the enigmatic love-hate-envy syndrome that people feel toward the Priscillas of the world. It's not just high-school snobs, it's grown-up dictatorial bosses, the arrogant rich, or the conceitedly beautiful. It first rears its ugly head when we're least able to understand or cope with it—in junior high and high school where *coolness* or *toughness* play a brief but significant role in our lives.[46]

At lunch I always sat with my best friend, Stella, and six or seven other members of my *Potluck*, a junior-high version of a sorority. On Friday nights we'd have Potluck Parties at a member's house where we brought food and gossiped until we heard our exasperated mothers honking their horns outside waiting to take us home. What did we talk about? Everything, but our favorite topic was Priscilla and her faithful followers.

On the school bus, the unspoken seating arrangement was very formalized. Prissy always sat in the second row back, window seat, nondriver's side. The entire first three rows were tacitly *reserved* for members of Prissy's cool clique. It was even considered bad taste for one of the *outsiders* to sit in the fourth row. That was tantamount to brazenly *auditioning* to be part of her elite circle. The only path to Prissy's prestigious entourage was to be befriended by the Princess or one of her closest ladies-in-waiting.

One windy, rainy day, Prissy was absent. The cool clique looked temporarily lost and leaderless. They didn't speak much to each other or to anyone else that day. It was if they were in mourning. Due to the torrential rain, the school bus was more crowded

MORE MAGNETIC ATTRACTION!

Rosa Parks did it. Joan of Arc did it. Julius Caesar did it. We all have the opportunities to be heroes or heroines in small ways by being the first to do something we believe in for our friends and loved ones, our people.

than usual on the trip home. A few standees were already huddled together and I was the last to board the packed bus. I was wet and tired, and only one empty seat remained: second row back, window seat, nondriver's side—Prissy's seat. One of the cool clique mob sat next to it jealously guarding it and smugly aware that she held the number two position even in Priscilla's absence. For a fleeting moment I flirted with courage. I looked first at the seat, then into the stony face of Prissy's seat guard, then up at my Potluck friends in the back of the bus. Did I imagine I heard Stella whispering, "Go, Leilie, go!"

I kept walking toward the back of the bus. A small part of me still regrets that moment.

Looking back at our American history, I have renewed respect for Rosa Parks, that courageous African-American woman who on Thursday, December 1, 1955, also a windy and rainy day, refused to relinquish her seat to a white man in the front of the bus. Looking back at my bus incident, I wonder what would have happened if I or one of the other outsiders sat in Prissy's seat and refused to budge. Would the rest of us nerds heroically band together and refuse to ride the bus to destroy the power grip of the clique? I think not. But we would have never forgotten the kid who had the guts to sit there.

♀♂

CLAUSE #26:

MY PERSONAL PRINCIPLES CLAUSE

When I *know* in my heart that something is right, I will go for it. Whether it's as important as racial relations or as insignificant as cracking a clique in one high school, I'll be the first to stand up—or sit down—for my folks. Yes, they'll like me for it. *But, most of all, I will like myself.* (And that's the first step to making everybody like me.)

31 Planting Seeds for New Friendships

Last year I made a trip to my old hometown because I had to take care of a small financial matter there. Three members of my old high-school Potluck still lived in town. We planned to each buy a few munchies for everybody and then get together that night just like we used to do so many years ago.

I went to the grocery store to pick up some fruit and cheese. I got in line with my goodies behind a big woman dressed in a cheap, wrinkled-cotton housecoat. She's the kind of woman that my country Uncle Charlie would say, "looked like she'd be plenty warm in winter and provide plenty of shade in the summer." Pushing her cart filled with food and two screaming kids, she jiggled forward a few shuffling steps every few minutes as the line got shorter.

One of her boys must have grabbed a candy bar from the checkout display because suddenly she lifted a hefty arm and cuffed him, slapping candy right out of his hand onto the floor. I immediately made a nosedive to pick it up to save her from what I knew would be a formidable undertaking. "The brat's up to his old tricks again," she explained as I handed it to her. "Thanks."

That voice! I'd never forget it. To confirm my suspicions, I looked into her face and there she was—a few more chins—but the same woman. It was Priscilla! Princess Priscilla who had ruled my high school with the same slightly sarcastic smile she was giving me now.

This time I looked at her not with envy but with sympathy and sadness. Not because of her weight. Not because of her rowdy kids. But because we just assume our superstars will go on and be superstars in everything they do in life. Priscilla's careworn face and crumpled clothes told me this was not the case.

My green-eyed monster died a quiet death.

Prissy's Present

That evening at Potluck, I told my old friends about my brief encounter with Prissy that afternoon. One of my Potluck pals had worked at the same insurance company with her after graduation. I asked Gina what happened. She blinked, obviously not having thought about Priscilla in a very long time.

"Well, after we graduated," Gina said, "I guess everyone sort of forgot about her. About half the girls in her clique went off to college. And to my knowledge, they didn't stay in touch. At least she didn't talk about it much."

"How long did Priscilla stay at GEICO?" I asked her.

"I don't know exactly," Gina continued, "because little by little the rest of us got promoted out of that department or moved on to better jobs. And Prissy just sort of stayed in the same position. Nobody really liked her at GEICO." At that point Gina laughed and said, "Her terror tactics didn't work in the real world."

Gina continued, "She started dating George, you know, the guy who owned the auto body shop next to Pops drugstore downtown. Then, I guess she got pregnant or something because they got married and pretty soon they had a baby. She quit GEICO and that was the last I heard of her. You said she's got two kids now?"

Gina asked the question quite dispassionately, a far cry from the reverent tone of voice we used whispering about the "Princess" in the halls. As we munched on our goodies, I found myself feeling a little sad for Priscilla.

You Can Never Go Back
(and Would You Really Want To?)

The subject soon changed to more pleasant subjects. I was thrilled to hear that Gina was now a senior rep at GEICO. She attributes her promotion to a friendship she formed at the company with a woman named Pamela, whom she called her mentor.

I begged Gina to tell me the story. She said, "Well, there was this woman that I always smiled at in the company lunchroom. She sort of reminded me of my mom. Anyway, one day when the cafeteria was full, she came over and asked if she could share my table. We had a really nice time and took to eating together practically every day.

"Well, I had no idea," Gina continued, "but soon I found out Pamela was married to a bigwig at the company, the head of personnel. Gradually she felt more comfortable with me, and she opened up and told me a lot of company inside dope."

You Made My Day!

"For example," Gina continued, "We had this system at GEICO, where if you did something nice for someone—you know, covered their phone for them while they were out or stayed late to help them finish a report—they'd give you a cute little blue card the company printed up that said, 'Thanks, you made my day!' and then they'd write the nice thing you did.

"It was good because it made us realize that people really appreciate the littlest things—like if a coworker was rushed, letting him or her ahead of you in the cafeteria line, or offering to lend a novel by an author you know he or she likes.

"Anyway, at the end of the day, we were supposed to drop it in the 'You Made My Day' box which I assumed was just for recycling purposes.

"But Pamela later told me that the cards were a big deal to the company. The personnel department emptied that box every week and put the cards into the employees' personnel records." Gina then proudly added that her mentor told her that Pamela had 120 "You Made My Day" cards in her file.

Gina then said, "Leil, you were asking about Prissy? Well, after she left, Pamela was clearing out her files and told me, confidentially, that Prissy didn't have even one card. That's probably why she never got promoted."

Now, About Your Promotion

Pretend that you are bucking for a promotion. (Of course you are. We all are, in everybody's eyes!) Every time you do a tiny favor for someone, no matter how small, a "You Made My Day" card is going into your personnel file. The more "You Made My Day" cards you have in your personnel file, the more people will like you. And isn't that what we're talking about here?

Since every workplace is different, every list will be different. List ten thoughtful things you can do for colleagues in your place of work that would earn you a card which says

"Thanks, You Made My Day for . . ."

1. _____

2. _____

3. _____

4. _____

5. _____

6. _____

7. _____

8. _____

9. _____

10. _____

♀♂

Clause #27:

Thanks, You Made My Day

I will keep my eye out at work and attempt to do some of the thoughtful things above for my colleagues.

✍ _____

---

32 Do You Want to Be Popular, or Do You Want to Be Liked?

Was Princess Priscilla popular at my high school? Most definitely yes. Was she genuinely liked? Most definitely no, certainly not by the majority of students. I sensed it then but was too young, too naive, or just too plain stupid to say it, even to myself. Decades later, when I started working with companies and exploring elements of charisma and authority, I realized I should have trusted my instinct. People genuinely liking you is a far cry from the Priscilla-type popularity that pervades many schools.

It wasn't until almost the turn of the millennium that researchers started studying popularity and cliques. Perhaps some of it was in response to a spate of high school tragedies and violence in response to social ostracism and unforgiving hierarchies in schools.

Teens on-line often bemoan the unfair rejection they receive from the "jocks" and "cool kids." I've read anguished messages such as "The popular conformists need to learn to accept everyone else. Why would they shun people who are different?"

"I can't even begin to say all the problems with cliques. I am seen as an outcast and dork by all of the popular people. . . . It hurts so much to be different."[47]

More Magnetic Attraction!

Crush the old popularity or unspoken social class system. It's outdated, outrageous, and should be outlawed. We can, to some degree, legislate against racial prejudice. However, *popularity prejudice* is so pervasive, people just close their eyes and pretend it doesn't exist. Unfortunately it does.

Reading messages like this, I find myself conjuring up painful pictures of being snubbed by the *in crowd* in my school. In those years, I saw my classmates as a microcosm of the world. And my acceptance or rejection by the cool clique seemed to me to be a harbinger of my acceptance or rejection in the real world. If only one member of the cool clique had been warm to me. If only one cool clique person had casually chatted with me while walking to class, or invited me to sit beside her on the bus, or joined our group at the lunch table, then I wouldn't have felt like such an outsider.

Did the teens who turned to savagery feel that they were doomed to be failures in life because the *jocks* and *cheerleaders* didn't accept them? Was the pain so great that they had to become violent? It will be a long time before we have answers to questions like this. But the important thing is, important people are starting to ask important questions.

And you and I can do important things, right now, in response to this ghastly wake-up call. As teenagers, as adults, as senior citizens, we can break the clique system, the cast system, the social snob system. Those at the bottom may even feel they can't bust it except perhaps by headline-exploding violence. But if you are at the top—say a cheerleader, a jock, a corporate giant, a member of *high society*, a celebrity, or a notable star in your galaxy of friends—then you can crack the clique system that exists at every level of life.

Look around your world, your company, your neighborhood. Don't you see someone who would value your friendship? Someone who perhaps the world would call unpopular, dorky, or freaky? Someone who is a little different from your other friends and whose life you could light up by shining on them. No one can honestly answer no to this question.

And, hey, you never know. The dorky looking guy with glasses and tousled hair whose nose is always pressed up against a computer screen. The girl with the big nose and long, stringy dishwater-blonde hair who goes around singing to herself. The chubby teen who always had a clever, cutting remark for everyone. Wouldn't it be great to have befriended those kids and now be able to count among your galaxy of friends Bill Gates, Barbra Streisand, or Roseanne?

And you know something? You'll find that the *nerd* enriches your life in many ways. You may not fall in love with your dweeb, but remember, legend has it that inside the frog is a handsome prince or beautiful princess just waiting to be freed by your kiss.

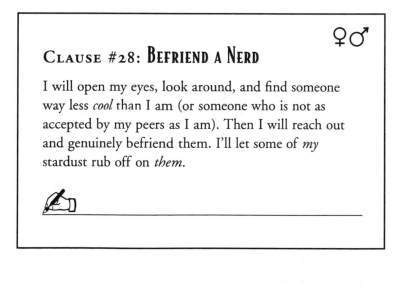

Clause #28: Befriend a Nerd

I will open my eyes, look around, and find someone way less *cool* than I am (or someone who is not as accepted by my peers as I am). Then I will reach out and genuinely befriend them. I'll let some of *my* stardust rub off on *them*.

33 What If I Only Feel Those Butterflies When I'm Talking to Him or Her?

Ah, now we're talking about a different puppy, a different diversity, yet another kind of minority, and it can be a very lonely one at that. We're talking about the drop-dead gorgeous people, the *tens*, both male and female.

"Ohh, poor things!" I can hear you say sarcastically.

No really, I have had several jobs where I had the good fortune—or miserable luck depending on how you look at it—of working with gorgeous people. There was a day in our not-so-ancient history when flight attendants had to meet a strict height, weight, and age (read *beauty*) requirement. Pan Am hired some token American women such as myself, but obviously the recruiters preferred the tall sexy Scandinavian beauties.

I became close friends with one of them, a knock-your-socks-off Swedish beauty from Stockholm. We flew together often. I witnessed men dropping coffee cups when they spotted her coming down the aisle. I saw twisting male heads one by one fall into the aisle like dominoes as she passed. I heard grown men, CEO types, rendered speechless when asked by Ulla to make the mind-boggling decision of whether to have coffee or tea. (She didn't say "or me" but you know they were thinking it.)

One would assume Ulla was deluged with dates, right? I know I did—until she told me the truth. Because she was so gorgeous, she intimidated men. No man likes to be turned down, and, to avoid that humiliation, very few had the courage to ask her out.

Ulla was not an isolated example. Years later when I ran a modeling agency, I heard the same thing repeatedly. The most beautiful women were often lonely because no one dared approach them.

Mother Nature played a dirty trick on us. The *more* we're attracted to someone, the *more* butterflies we have in our stomach when talking to that terrific him or her. That unfortunate fact was proved by a study called "Shyness and Physical Attractiveness in Mixed-Sex Dyads" (just a fancy way of saying man-woman two-somes).[48] Researchers and self-appointed experts on attractiveness, ruthlessly gave a control group of people who didn't know each other a rating on their looks. The men ranged from matinee-idol handsome all the way down to a few who . . . well, if you looked up *ugly* in a dictionary, you'd find their pictures. Likewise the women ranged from drop-dead gorgeous all the way down to some who were critically beauty-challenged.

Then the researchers went about their work of introducing each man to each woman, meanwhile registering their heartbeats, sweaty palms, breathing rates—in other words, counting the but-terflies in their stomachs. The results? The more attractive the

MORE MAGNETIC ATTRACTION!

Studies prove the *tens* can be pretty lonely people because no one figures they measure up. So take a shot. If you are attracted to a *ten*, let him or her know. Your chances are much better than you think. If nothing else, it will destroy the butterflies when talking with the *normal-looking* folks!

partner, the more shy and flustered the opposite-sex stranger meeting him or her was.

Conversely, the subjects were calm, cool, and collected, and the butterflies didn't flap a wing for either men or women when they met the less attractive opposite-sex subjects. Who said life was fair?

Great, So I Know Why. Now How Can I Get Rid of Those Butterflies?

Unfortunately, there's no Raid or Roach Motel (like the ad sadistically says, "They check in, but they don't check out") for the butterflies in your tummy. However, armed with a little knowledge, you'll feel a lot more confident becoming a friend or lover with a *ten*.

It has been shown that it is not our actual attractiveness, but our *perception* of our own attractiveness that plays the major role. In one study, ninety-nine people were told that they were being rated for attractiveness.[49] Then researchers gave them totally incorrect information. They told some of the lesser attractive people they had rated them very highly, and vice versa. (What a blow to your ego to think you're attractive and then hear you're a dud! However, far be it from me to argue the ethics of science.)

Then, in a supposedly unrelated experiment, the researchers told everyone to choose a partner for a task. Practically everyone chose a partner whom they thought was essentially just as attractive *as they thought they had been judged to be*, not as they really were. In fact, results showed that the opinion they had received about their own attractiveness was the primary factor that determined who they chose, especially when it came to choosing someone of the opposite sex. Even in this small microcosm, the adage "we are what we think the world thinks we are" seemed to reign.

Especially in dating, if a man or woman only feels like a *five*, he or she is going to be uncomfortable making overtures to the *tens*. The typical thought pattern of a man afraid of rejection is, "Oh, gosh, she's so beautiful. I bet every guy tries to talk to her. She'll think I'm just another one of those jerks if I try to make the approach." Women also hesitate to fall into a relationship with an extraordinarily good-looking man because they assume, given all his opportunity, he would be a womanizer.

Research has proved that people usually wind up with someone who is within a two-point range of themselves in attractiveness. That could be because most people are afraid to approach the extremely handsome men or beautiful women. Ulla told me, but it took the results of the studies to prove it to me that, *tens* can be very lonely people indeed.

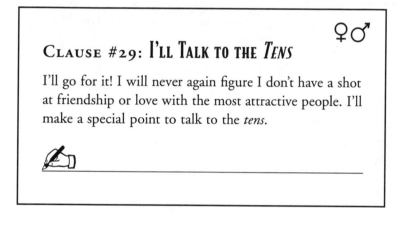

Clause #29: I'll Talk to the *Tens*

I'll go for it! I will never again figure I don't have a shot at friendship or love with the most attractive people. I'll make a special point to talk to the *tens*.

34 Have You Ever Had a Friend...

Who Changed Your Way of Looking at Life Forever?

I mean really changed it—the way you see certain people and situations forever? I've been fortunate enough to have shared moments with two such friends, and, tragically, they had something in common. Devastating accidents had left both with major disabilities.

Soon after I moved to New York, I attended a concert and happened to sit next to a striking young woman named Leslie who was also there alone. She and I started chatting and hit it off instantly. The band was not that terrific, and we joked about getting together and starting our own all-girl group. We weren't serious about that, but since we were both new to New York and had few friends here, we were serious about wanting to get together.

When the concert was over, our chatting wasn't and we found ourselves the last ones in the theater. I invited her over to my place the following week and happened to mention that she better do her exercises, because I lived in a three-flight walk-up. She laughed and suggested we meet at a nearby coffee shop that she happened to know instead.

I jumped up to grab my coat, and it was only then that I noticed Leslie wasn't standing. Instead, she was deftly lifting herself from the theater chair to a wheelchair that I hadn't seen parked in the aisle. I wanted to die inside about my three-flight walk-up comment, but it apparently hadn't affected her.

The following Saturday morning, I arrived early at our appointed place, and right on time, Leslie wheeled up. We laughed and joked all the way through our breakfast. When the check came, she dove into her bag with one hand and said, "Oh, please let me."

No, no, I said reaching across the table and grabbing her other arm—which felt like rubber! She must have noticed my astonished expression because she just smiled and said, "Don't worry, Leil, now you've discovered all my false parts."

Very matter of factly, she went on to tell me about the accident which had severed her right arm and rendered her right leg practically useless. She told me that she and her then boyfriend who had a small Cessna 150 plane were going for a Sunday outing. Just as he was about to rev up the engines, she remembered that she'd left her purse in the tiny terminal in front of the plane. She stepped down from the plane and ran toward the terminal. Just at the wrong moment, the propellers started and sliced Leslie's lower arm off. The freak accident flipped her over, the propeller came around again and sliced through all the nerves in her leg.

The slings and arrows of outrageous fortune had left their mark on Leslie's body—but what had they done to her psyche? How does a beautiful woman adjust to life as a cripple, the horrible designation that some thoughtless people use? I didn't dare ask nor did she speak any more about her accident or the impact on her. She gracefully changed the subject and said that next week she'd love to see my loft if I'd help her up the stairs.

That was the beginning of a long friendship that lasted many years. Leslie did fulfill her dream of becoming a singer, at least part-time. During those years we went to countless concerts, movies, plays, and social events together. I attended the opening night each time she was booked at a new club. At each, I could view the world through her eyes.

This was before the Americans with Disabilities Act was passed, and we had to call every theater and every restaurant we went to to find out if a wheelchair could enter. We had to call every club to ask if the ladies' room was on the same floor. We had to look at every sink to see if it was low enough for her to wash her hands, or if it had a mirror low enough to check her makeup before going on stage—or whether she would only see the top of her head. Seeing the world from a wheelchair is a very different perspective.

If Leslie had just one wish in the world, it would be to be *normal*. Once she told me that without a thought, she would trade places with the humblest able bodied (AB) woman in the world. Her signature song almost always moved her audience to tears. It was an old Carole King song popularized by Aretha Franklin, "Cause you make me feel, you make me feel, you make me feel like a natural woman."

Leslie taught me that people with disabilities hate not being treated "natural." They enjoy casual conversation with strangers as much as anyone else. She said, don't just think of us as *handicapped* or *disabled*. Think person first, disability second. "After that minor brain tune-up," she said, "even your language will change. You'll be saying *person with a disability*, not a *handicapped person*. You'll say *visually impaired*, not *blind person*; or *hearing impaired*, not *deaf person*. You'll talk about someone *in a wheelchair*, not a *wheelchair-bound person*."

I once asked her if people should ignore someone's disability.

"No, it's obvious to us that it's obvious to you," she said. "But let us take the lead in talking about it. We will when we feel comfortable."

♡ More Magnetic Attraction!

Having a physically challenged (PC) friend will open new worlds for you. Your PC pal may become the most wonderful friend you'll ever have because he or she had to travel so much farther than most. You'll never see the world in quite the same way again. You'll experience emotions you never thought possible.

Leslie said one question she despises is, "What happened to you? Were you born with . . ." But, she said if you ask the same question in a different way, we're happy to tell you. Just say how did you come upon your disability? Have you had your disability since birth? This treats the disability as something we wear or have, not as an integral part of us.

Leslie gave me one of the most beautiful compliments I've ever received—one, unfortunately I knew I didn't deserve. One evening in a little club where she was singing, as she finished her signature song, she looked at me and said into the microphone, "I want to dedicate that song to my friend Leil. Because she makes me feel like a natural woman."

I didn't keep many secrets from Leslie during the years of our friendship. However, I never told her that had I known when I first met her so many years ago that she was in a wheelchair and had only one arm, I probably would not have been as comfortable chatting and joking with her. I would have been frozen like so many others when confronting someone with a disability. And our beautiful friendship never would have happened.

The Leslie story ends happily. She fell in love with a man who played the piano for her at one of her club acts. Within the year they married and moved to St. Thomas where Leslie and her husband are one of the most popular club acts on the island.

My friendship with Leslie paved the way for a light flirtation I had with an engineer at a studio where I was recording some of my audio tapes. The receptionist had already taken me into the recording booth when his voice came through on my earphones welcoming me and asking me if I was ready to start.

I made the usual number of recording bloopers, and he gently guided me through all of them. I liked his voice, and, although I couldn't see him too clearly through the double recording glass, I could see that he had some facial scarring. His silhouette intrigued me. He had long hair halfway down his back, and, in the distance, he looked like—don't laugh—Fabio, the heartthrob on the cover of many Harlequin romances.

After the session, I went out to meet him, and I could see that it wasn't just a few scars. His entire face was badly scarred and distorted. Obviously he had undergone many plastic surgery operations to try to construct an almost entirely new face which looked like it had been badly burned.

We chatted for a few minutes, and I asked him if, after the recording session, he happened to be driving in the direction of my hotel. He was, and on the way, I suggested we grab a bite at a restaurant we were passing. He seemed surprised at my invitation and haltingly agreed.

During dinner, struggling to sound as though his question were casual, he asked why his distorted face had not turned me off. I told him, truthfully, that it had not. In fact I saw tremendous beauty in his eyes.

Then when I mentioned that someone I had come to deeply admire was a man who not only had worse burns than he but was also in a wheelchair, he asked in awe, "Do you know W. Mitchell?" I said yes, I had been fortunate enough to meet him several times at a National Speakers Association conference. A flaming motorcycle accident had taken W. Mitchell's face, his fingers, and nearly his life. Later, in an emergency crash landing in his private plane, he was paralyzed and confined to a wheelchair. Now W. Mitchell is tougher on his wheelchair tires than he is on himself. He travels the world delivering his inspiring message that, as one of his books is titled, *It's Not What Happens to You, It's What You Do About It.*[50]

W. Mitchell was Richard's hero, and my connection with him, however slight, was all he needed. His emotional and verbal floodgates opened. The fact that I knew W. Mitchell somehow gave him permission to pour his soul out on a subject he rarely, if ever, spoke to anyone about. He told me the story of the car crash which killed his mother and burned 90 percent of his body when he was only three. He told me of his years of suffering as a child, and the gradual and ghastly realization that he looked different from everybody else. He told me how he knew people were *repulsed by the monster*, and how they would point and stare. He detailed dozens of painful incidents—how his father beat up a man in a grocery store when he overheard the man whispering to his kid about the *freak* in the next aisle, how his own brother didn't want to be seen walking to school with him, how in his entire life he'd only had a handful of dates and he knew those were *sympathy* dates and the women felt sorry for him.

I tried to convince Richard that he had a very special quality and that many women, including myself, found him very attractive. But Richard's pain was too great and his experiences too poignant, to ever have a relationship with a woman unless separated by the double glass at the studio. Maybe if he someday hears W. Mitchell tell his story, "The Man Who Would Not Be Defeated,"[51] he will.

Or perhaps his mind will travel back to my descriptions of the gorgeous women I've seen wheeling W. Mitchell around the National Speakers Association conference.

♀♂

CLAUSE #30:

MY PHYSICALLY CHALLENGED PAL

If I know someone with a physical challenge, I will become closer to him or her. Also I will actively seek out the friendship of other physically challenged pals.

✍ _____

35 If You've Got It, Flaunt It!

After the dark dungeon which imprisoned me for four months mysteriously dissolved, I was able to peek back through the bars and see that I would not have survived if it had not been for my two dear friends, Giorgio and Phil. It was at that moment I resolved to meet more people, all types of people.

Phil and I decided to give a series of "Bimonthly Meet New People Parties." We invited a dozen or so friends and invited each to bring someone along, the more unusual the better (although we didn't say it in precisely those terms).

The word *diversity* was an understatement describing that first bash. A seventy-year-old retired corporate giant chatting with an orange-haired kid with a Mohawk didn't turn any of the other party goers' heads. Conversation ranged from the stock market to the flea market, rock music to muzak, jogging to logging.

People often ask me, "Who was the most unusual person at the party?" It was a close call, but I'd have to say "Nicky the Nose" would get the dubious honor. If ever you should hear someone attacking insurance sales people as uncreative, you can counter with the fact that they have come up with every kind of insurance policy imaginable. Insuring people's houses, cars, and health is nothing. They offer doctors and lawyers, of course, malpractice insurance. They sell companies *bad rumor* insurance. Virtuoso insurance agents determine what esoteric value entities have to certain folks. Then agents offer expensive personalized policies so those paranoid people can sleep at night.

For example, surgeons who don't even like to shake hands for fear of finger crunching, take out policies on their hands. Betty Grable started the trend of actresses insuring their legs. My friend Pam, the actress, brought a fellow performer who had a two-million-dollar policy on his nose to our party.

Why his nose? Because this particular *performer* makes his entire living on his schnoz. Nicholas is one of the few, if not the only actor, who can—right on cue—let out a huge achoo, a medium honk, or a little toot. His clients can choose *with sniffle sounds* signifying the common cold, or *dry* signifying the beginning of a cold. In fact one cold-remedy company tried to sign him on as an exclusive. But, as my friend likes to tell it, "The nose knows." He turned up his well-trained one at their offer. Instead he sneezes on command with just the right tone and nasality for the highest bidder's price.

Nicky the Nose's nasal talents don't end there. It is as though his proboscis is double-jointed. He can turn it up, down, right, or left. He can flare his nostrils so he looks like a pig, or squeeze them so tight he looks like he has was born with a silver pince-nez on his schnoz.

It was very cold the night of the party. Pam arrived with Nicky who had a cashmere scarf around the lower half of his face guarding his sole source of income from the elements. I put out my hand to welcome him to the party. Instead of shaking hands, however, he gave a respectful little bow and was seated; Pam, seeing my puzzled look, explained that Nicholas never shook hands for fear of cold germs and always protected his nose from the elements.

I asked Nicky what movies and commercials he'd been in, and he promptly listed an impressive array of pharmaceutical companies who make cold remedies. He said those were just for his

♡ MORE MAGNETIC ATTRACTION!

When baby boomers were little more than babies, they sat in schoolroom classes watching a series of films on how to *fit in* and *be like everyone else*. Nowadays, the People Magnet who has the courage to stand out and be different is the one we respect and admire. The People Magnet who nose, er knows, his or her assets and plays them up wins our hearts. Like Nicky's nose, something about you can stand out.

sneeze, his sniffle, and his whiz. (He seemed to know the difference.) He had also done commercials for nose drops, nose-hair clippers, and a nose clip for swimmers that conforms to the shape of any nose. He told us one of his favorites was a TV spot for a national newspaper. While the announcer asked, "Do you have a nose for news?" Nick's nose tip traveled left to right, appearing to read.

By this time, a small group of party goers had gathered around this masked storyteller. Then, slowly unveiling his treasure, he announced that it had finally broken into the fragrance industry. He seemed quite fond of one suggestive TV ad he had filmed the week before. The commercial opened with a closeup of his nose only a few millimeters away from a shapely female bosom overflowing from a white silk evening gown. As the voice-over said, "Don't wear just any perfume," Nick's nose-tip took a downward dip. The voice-over continued with "Excite him with . . ." and here was the product name. At this point, the tip of Nicky's nose stood tall, virile, and erect. When the camera pulled back, the gorgeous female winked at the camera as the handsome sniffer's strong arms encircled her, and he buried his face in the valley of her hilly terrain.

Except now, Nick wasn't the male. They used a handsome actor who happened to have a similar looking nose. In fact, Nick didn't seem the least bit sensitive to the fact that they used another actor for the full-body shot.

You see, Nick didn't consider himself the *stand-in nose* for the handsome actor. In fact, he referred to the actor in the final shot as a stand-in for his significant sniffer.

Nicky then began to give us an unsolicited tour of his notorious nose pointing out the nares, dorsum, and philitrm along the way. I decided it was crossing the bounds of good taste to let us hear his famous sneeze. After all, meeting Maria Callas at a party, one would not ask for an aria. Meeting Gregory Hines, one wouldn't ask for a little tap dance.

But Nicky the Nose must have sensed my desire because, just then, he began a long wheezy three-second inhale and then let out a thunderous *ah-chooo* which sounded as though it could blow the windows out of our loft. Everyone at the party froze. It was as though a huge freight train had just come through the loft. Never again will I think of those insipid little noises we mere mortals make when we have a cold or a sneeze. In fact, Nicky did carry a two-million-dollar disability policy on it—"disability" defined in his policy as the inability of his nose to "perform."

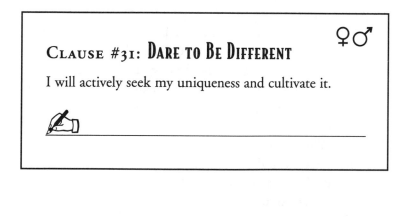

CLAUSE #31: DARE TO BE DIFFERENT ♀♂

I will actively seek my uniqueness and cultivate it.

36 Diversity, It's Not Just for the Workplace

In 1945 or so, Saint Peter, hearing a ruckus on earth, looked down from the heavens on high, then turned to Jesus and said, "My Lord, listen to all that bawling, bellering, and booming down there. They're multiplying like rabbits!"

And Jesus replied, "Yes, Peter, let them be known as *baby boomers*." And so they were.

Then Jesus continued, "And, Pete, I want to warn you. When they get to your gates, they're going to have a lot of stories to tell. Those boomers are going to behold more of life as a group than any of their brothers and sisters before them. Some of the things they'll see will be good—and long overdue, I must say. They'll give the good ones names like *civil rights movement* and *women's liberation*. They'll also see some stuff that has a good side and a bad side. They'll call them *student activism* and *sexual revolution*. A couple of them will even take a few baby steps toward us up here with the rest of them watching on TV. Of course they'll call them *giant steps for mankind.*

"All these happenings the boomers will experience together will create a fantastic fellowship among them. But, I'll tell you Pete, in my eyes, the biggest step will not be that guy Armstrong's on the moon. It will be when they start appreciating the incredible diversity I gave them."

Perhaps, in the eyes of God, diversity was the biggest step mankind has ever taken.

Guess Who's Coming to Dinner?

Until the early 1950s, that question, "Guess who's coming to dinner?", would strike fear in Mummy and Daddy's heart. Many baby boomers were the first in their family to bring home a friend of a different color.

But now that baby boomers are parents, many look forward to their teenagers playing the "Guess who's coming . . ." game. They know whoever shares their table that evening will probably be able to broaden their understanding of the world. Many of their own friendships, some of which have spanned three decades, are cross-cultural.

Sometimes we become confused, and, instead of listening to our hearts, we listen to the heartless. I was on the front end of the baby boomers, and the world was a very different place then. Civil rights was in our recent history books, but it wasn't flowing through our veins yet.

In my high-school class, there were six African-American girls. One of them, Lacey, had been sent by her family in Bermuda to study in the States. Lacey's locker was next to mine and, daily, as we crammed stuff in and yanked stuff out of our lockers, she and I would talk nonstop. I spent summers in Bermuda because my mom, a speech pathologist, worked there tutoring a little girl who was the daughter of a Member of the Bermudian parliament and his wife. Whenever we talked about Bermuda, she'd get homesick, and I'd get nostalgic. Sometimes we'd talk about how we missed Bermuda until we were almost in tears, and then we'd break out hugging each other and laughing together.

One day, as we were chatting by our lockers just before lunch, it came up that Lacey knew the man whose daughter my mom tutored. She said there had been some heated debates in the

Bermudian parliament recently because some of the MPs thought "Negroes should not be hired as sales clerks in the Front Street shops."

"Why not?" I asked her naively.

"Because they think it will turn tourists off."

That's strange, I remember thinking. But we both laughed it off and then I didn't think much more about it.

Far more interesting to me, in those days, was Lacey's description of the dating scene in Bermuda. She gave me the names of some places where the locals went to meet each other. We continued our girl talk about this all the way to the lunchroom. I wanted to write down some of the names of the Bermudian hot spots she'd mentioned, so I invited Lacey to join me and some of the Potluck girls at our table.

She smiled, politely declined, and said, "No, but you're certainly welcome to sit with us if you like." Without thinking anything about it, I went and sat with Lacey and several of her black Bermudian friends. We launched into a hot discussion about places like The Swizzle Inn, Bailey's Ice Cream Parlor, The White Horse Tavern, and several I'd never heard of.

More Magnetic Attraction!

People Magnets know how lonely someone feels when the majority of people around them are a different nationality or a different color. No matter where you live, "The Black Experience," "The White Experience," "The Asian Experience," "The Hispanic Experience," and the "Your First Is My Second Language Experience" are very different. Fortunately, if you make friends with someone who has a thick accent in today's world, nobody will whisper. They'll just admire you for walking what, unfortunately, most people just talk.

Just as I was scribbling down the names, one of my Potluck girls came over and whispered something in my ear. I was stunned. My Potluck mate had said, "Leil, everyone in the lunchroom is looking at you. You shouldn't be sitting here." Feigning unawareness that I was being chided because I was sitting at "the Negroes table," my Bermudian friends started talking among themselves. Behind my hand, I said to my Potluck mate, "Why?"

She just rolled her eyes and said, "Leil, you know" and went back to *our* table. Finally it dawned on me. I smiled at my Bermudian friends and tried to pick up the discussion where it left off. But I could tell that things were different now. Conversation was strained.

Another moment that I am now ashamed to remember is that I never joined Lacey and her friends at the lunchroom table again. Lacey and I remained fast locker friends, but that was it.

However, a few weeks later, Carolyn, not exactly one of the cool clique, but close to it, made a move that astounded the whole school. She started being seen walking the halls with Lacey and standing outside the school on warm days chatting with Lacey and her black friends. At first many of my schoolmates whispered, in that tone usually reserved for scandals, about their friendship. But, as Carolyn and Lacey were seen together more and more, even sitting next to each other in study hall—people stopped talking. Deep down, I think everyone realized that what Carolyn was doing was really cool, and the rest of the students were very wrong to think anything of it.

Little by little, people's opinions started reversing themselves. And by the time Carolyn found herself once or twice a week sitting at Lacey's table, the rejection of Carolyn had turned openly to respect of her.

I, too, admired Carolyn. But I had a sadness and a shame mixed with my admiration. I should have been that girl who broke the insidious unspoken rule. I should have been the girl to make the first obvious and flaunted cross-racial friendship in our school. I should have known that my friendship with Lacey was far more important than what a few misguided people thought about me.

Since then I have made many cross-cultural friendships. I've learned how to cook couscous from a Tunisian friend and how to take 2 hours and 45 minutes to pour and drink one cup of tea from a Japanese friend. I've gone to a jai alai match with a Mexican friend; watched grown men hyperventilate over throwing a metal ball around in the sand (the game of Petanque) with an Italian; and I even saw a guy catch a cow with three pieces of twine and a ball (a bola) with an Argentine friend. What have I done for them? Well, I've introduced them all to McDonalds hamburgers, country music, and Thanksgiving turkey.

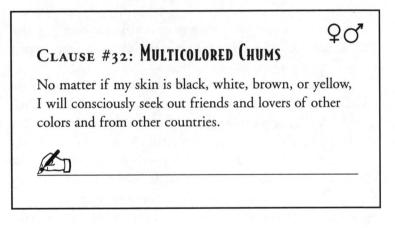

CLAUSE #32: MULTICOLORED CHUMS

No matter if my skin is black, white, brown, or yellow, I will consciously seek out friends and lovers of other colors and from other countries.

PART FOUR

CUPID'S SECRETS

*Sexy Schemes for Luring Lovers
and Keeping Them*

37 Cupid's Got *Lots* of Secrets!

See if you can answer this riddle:

> It's impossible to describe.
> It's more common than the common cold (and
>   sometimes can be more of a nuisance).
> It comes and goes with no apparent reason.
> We have no idea what brings it on,
> And when it goes, it's almost impossible to get back.
> We have no idea why it happens.
> Lots of times you expect it, and it never happens.
> Other times it happens and you didn't expect it.
> Sometimes you welcome it.
> Sometimes it gets in your way.
> There is no predicting when or where it will hit,
> But it usually comes in a flash—
> Then it disappears just as fast.
> Or sometimes it dies an agonizingly long, slow
>   painful death.

It's one word. What is it?

If you guessed *love*, some people would say, "You're close." Others would laugh and say, "You're way off base! It has nothing to do with love." Since this perplexing phenomenon is so common and hits everybody at some time or another, linguists had to give it a name. But nobody could pin it down. So they wound up giving it a name that seemed virtually worthless at the time. They called it *chemistry*.

Cupid, Please Tell Me, Why Him? Why Her?

We've all asked ourselves the same question. "It seems crazy. Of all the people in the world, why do I find this one person so attractive? Why do the sparks fly when we're together, and not when I'm with anyone else—even though that 'anyone else' is much better looking?"

Women, for us, *chemistry* seems even crazier. Imagine ten men are standing in a row like a police lineup. Instead of having to choose which one is guilty of burglary, you have to choose which, if any, is guilty of a different type of robbery—stealing your heart at first sight. You look at each, one by one. They're all good-looking guys, but no suspects yet. You're getting near the end of the line. The policewoman in attendance is about to dismiss the men because nobody would ever believe that funny-looking, tall lanky cowboy at the end of the line with the smiling eyes, the sarcastic smile, and the lock of hair falling in his face could be the one.

Then you take one glance at him and, *blam*! There goes your heart. Why?

When Two of Cupid's Arrows Cross

Before we answer that, we should probably discuss some fantasies, falsehoods, and facts about love at first sight. Suppose the cowboy looks at you and finds you "purdy as a little red heifer in a flowerbed." His big doofy heart skips a beat too. Before a word is spoken, you both know you are destined to ride off into the sun-set together.

Is it possible? Does love at first sight exist? What do you think?

Let's put it this way. It exists if the two of you agree that's what it was. It exists if, six months later you're sitting on the couch together holding hands and cooing to all your friends, "It was love at first sight." Nobody—not even those cold-hearted scientists I cite—want to burst your balloon.

All of this is just to say that *love at first sight* is merely a semantic term that covers that delicious serendipity when two people look at each other and feel a simultaneous *blam*. Then the *double blam* turns into a serious relationship.[52]

Nothing beats love at first sight . . . except maybe love with *insight*.

Some Cupids Who Crashed and Burned

Back to *why*. Starting with Aristotle and Plato, right on up through the heyday of psychoanalysis (with Wilhelm Reich telling us that love is "filling a void in oneself," and Sigmund Freud not really believing that sometimes a cigar is just a cigar—it's *always* sex!), there have been countless theories as to why our little hearts go pitty-patty when we look at one opposite sex (usually) indi-vidual and not another.

The most recent theory to bite the dust is Margaret Mead's. This superstar anthropologist observed the mind-boggling antics of males and females the world over and told us that all this sex stuff was learned. It's the old nature versus nurture argument, and she cast her vote on the nurture side.

"We may safely say," she wrote, "that many if not all of the personality traits which we call masculine and feminine are as lightly linked to sex as are the clothing, the manners, and the form of headdress that a society at a given period assigns to sex."[53]

Her colleagues later proved Margie factually wrong, but she had been 100 percent politically correct because the times were ready for such a feminist theory. It benefited our fair sex for the world to think there was little difference between homo sapien males and homo sapien females. (At least it helped women smash a few glass ceilings and take the wind out of a few old windbag politicians.)

Before the argument got too lodged, however, some vehement scientists hopped aboard the love boat and found that a large body of research on specific behavior could not possibly, as Mead had proposed, be traced to learning. Even when children are brought up in identical isolated environments, little boys will still bop each other on the head, and little girls will still try to diaper the cat.

Upon further examination, they found that there were, indeed, biological factors that contributed to these behaviors. There were differing levels of sex hormones and even sex-specific differences in the human brain.[54] The prevailing theory now was that men and women are very different. (*"Mais alors"* say the French. But of course. *"Vive la difference!"*)

Speaking practically for a moment, it's unfortunate that, when the good Lord gave us male and female brains, respectively, He didn't include an information kit for the one we didn't get. We'll try to make up for some of that here.

38 Finally Science Captures Cupid

At last the world of science has found *the* explanation of love that is tough to refute because, like pieces of a tight puzzle, it fits in all disciplines from anthropology to zoology.

Scientists have isolated chemicals in our brain called neurotransmitters. They are responsible for that wonderful wacky feeling of being in love, wanting to shout it from the rooftops, singing about it in the rain, and doing a variety of looney things dangerous to life and limb. Now the neurotransmitter that really causes grown men and women to come unglued and want to swing from the chandeliers can be traced specifically to the one called phenylethylamine (PEA).[55]

Our PEA-soaked lovesick brain causes grown men to talk baby talk, and grown women to count the hairs on their lover's chest. It causes us to think our love object is the center of the universe and that even the most mundane and trivial characteristic of our magical other is a source of utter fascination.[56]

Cupid Does Drugs

Now this PEA substance, along with the two other natural amphetamines, dopamine and norepinephrine, which floods our lovesick brains, has some other debatable side effects. We feel giddy, optimistic, wonderfully alive, and full of extraordinary energy, and we want to dance or make love all night in a euphoric trance. In other words, we're stoned out of our gourds!

"Hey what's so bad about that?" you ask. Well, nothing—for a short period of time. However, like any drug, it takes its toll. You'd crash if you were constantly high. Not only that, but like any drug, you can become addicted to it. In fact, some people are. They get comfortable in a really good relationship, but, unfortunately, the newness, the excitement, the PEA wears off. So these folks blame it on the relationship and think it's going stale.

They deserve your sympathy. They are uninformed and sick. We call them *love junkies* because they jump from one relationship to the next in an attempt to keep that initial high going all the time. Or they keep the excitement going by continually getting themselves in bad or abusive relationships.

Why Do So Many Women Go for the Bad Boys?

A constant quandary for men is why some women are attracted to the tough bad boys. It isn't just women. Many men also find themselves getting entangled in costly relationships. Admittedly it is confusing because people profess to wanting a nice partner but continually get themselves in destructive relationships. Why?

There are several theories. The most plausible is that they find a perverse kind of pleasure in this type of liaison. Many women find abusive men attractive because, to all outward appearances, they seem confident. They give off the air of knowing what they want and pushing others around to get it. Usually it covers up a deep insecurity, but many of these *tough* guys keep it deeply hidden.

It also could be that the tough guy reminds her of a time when she was a little girl. Daddy may have pushed her around, but she knew that deep down he loved her. Thus she connects the being pushed around with being loved.

Additionally, as they grow up, many people feel their life lacks drama. They remember the pain, the pleasure, the discovery, the being on the brink of disaster of their first love. Later, they develop a *been there, done that* attitude with relationships, and they have a higher and higher threshold of what it takes to get that PEA juice flowing again. For some, it gets to the point where they have to be abused in order to recapture those melodramatic moments and get their PEA jolt.

The results of a massive study of women who continually chose abusive partners revealed that they suffered low self-esteem. The relationship only aggravated it. The verbal aggression and violence they endured caused depression and a myriad of other symptoms. Yet they stayed. Many were love dependent, feeling that they could not survive without the partner's love.

It is very common for women who love a bad boy to have a nice guy waiting in the wings—a soft bed to fall on if the tough guy gets too tough. They keep stringing their nice boy along as an insurance policy.

Researchers call this phenomenon of being attracted to the bad boys, "The Stockholm Syndrome," and it is very difficult, if not impossible, for a *nice guy* to pull her out of it. Many *nice guys* in my seminar ask me if they should stay in the wings in the hope she'll see the light?

I answer, "Your choice, but the statistics are pretty bleak. It must be *her* desire to escape the repetitive destructive pattern, and, deep down, she probably doesn't want to."

Cupid Grows Up

The hot, passionate kind of love, in other words, the state of *abnormality* caused by PEA promotes mating. However, after this, remaining this high is not evolutionarily advantageous. It's bad for the eventual offspring. Given the crazy things lovers do, that could threaten survival of the kids' parents. (They could fall while shouting their love from the rooftop, or catch pneumonia while singing in the rain about it.) Speaking biologically, unless unusual circumstances (three of which we'll soon discuss) intervene, the PEA subsides.

Bye-bye PEA, bye-bye love. So goes the PEA, so goes the relationship—in many other cultures as well. Anthropologist Helen Fisher found that in societies as varied as Russia, Egypt, South Africa, Venezuela, and Finland, divorces generally occur the year after the PEA disappears from their system, and the reality of two very different biological animals (male and female) having to deal with each other sets in.[57]

So How Long Can I Enjoy this Legal High Before I Come Down?

Here's the answer you've been waiting for. The normal life-span of PEA is one and a half to three years.[58] Sorry, but it's true. The first happy, happy days and hot, hot nights last, on the average, only up to three years.

Still, it doesn't make sense that couples split just because of a PEA drain. It does *not* mean anything is wrong with the relationship! It just means that nature is taking its natural course for propagation of the species. The great PEA loss is much better for the kids and the long-range good of you and your spouse.

Since parents must care for children well into their teen years, Mother Nature doesn't want you to separate and have the kids shuttled back and forth. But, if she leaves you with a PEA-filled brain, you might be copulating around the clock when you need to take the kids to the doctor or get them ready for school. Or all the couples in the neighborhood would be shouting their love from the rooftops all night long and the kids couldn't get any sleep.

39 A Better, Deeper Kind of Love Sets in, Really!

So Mother Nature gives us another gift, one that unfortunately, many people don't appreciate. The brain compensates by increasing the levels of morphinelike substances, endorphins.[59] These create feelings of calm, security, well-being—that *family kind of love*. Wait, there's more good news. If you open your heart to this new kind of love, it will give you the deeply satisfying lifetime of love that we all crave.

Passionate love turns into companionate love. Eros goes from illogical need and obsession to mutual support and acceptance. Any way you look at it, it's a much classier pooch than puppy love.

What if You *Still* Want the "Can't Wait to Jump Your Bones" Kinda Love?

Well, for those of you who just have to have it, there is one way to keep the hot puppy barking. But not with your partner.

The first is having the spouse for the forever kind of family love—and the occasional lover on the side for the hot 'n' heavy stuff. However that would make you a two-timing, sneakin' deacon, double-crossing, two-faced, hanky-panky philanderer who risks losing the long-lasting kind of love that nature intended you to have and is proven to give you the most happiness over time. If that's what you want, that's your business, but I don't recommend it.

By the way, here's a statistic for those of you who think you're missing out on something that everybody else has: based on interviews with a random sample of almost 3,500 people, ages 18–59, the Social Organization of Sexuality found that the average American male has sex with six women over a lifetime, and the average American woman has only two lovers.[60] When they counted noses on hanky-panky, 75 percent of married men and 85 percent of married women had never put their nose on the same pillow with anyone but their spouse.

Is there a way I can keep the passion flower blooming with one partner? Yes, but it may not be worth the effort. Let me tell you about a friend of mine, Cindy, who has managed to keep her marriage hot and sexy for almost four years now. That's almost a record for PEA duration.

How Cindy Keeps the Sex Cinders Hot

Perhaps you remember Cindy from earlier in this book or from *How to Make Anyone Fall in Love with You*. She was my nail technician (I still have trouble not saying "manicurist") and was forever complaining that, in her line of work, she never met any men. And, after a long day of nail filing, buffing, and clipping hangnails, she was too tired to go out and socialize.

Although Cindy didn't have a boyfriend, she did have a platonic male friend, Victor, a carpenter who occasionally helped Cindy when she needed some repairs around the salon. I could never figure out why she let him hang around because, every time I had my nails done, Cindy regaled me with some new horror that Victor had committed.

Once she told me that the previous week, she stayed after hours to give him a manicure. He's always bragged how "tough as a cactus" he was, but when clipping his hangnails, she happened to give him a teensy cut.

"You should have heard him squeal," Cindy said. "Then, he had the nerve to call me clumsy! I was furious, I suggested he finish his own %#! manicure.

"So instead of saying he's sorry for snapping, he gets up, goes over, and turns on the TV, and clams up. Typical male," she muttered.

Another time, Cindy said, "Victor came into the salon at one of our busiest times to repair a broken lighting fixture. All the girls and I were rushing around taking care of our clients. So Victor works on the light in silence for about fifteen minutes, and then as he's leaving, instead of saying something nice to me, he says to all with a big grin on his puss, 'Boy oh boy. You gals can sure talk up a storm. I think you all were vaccinated with phonograph needles. Hardy har har.' And that, in front of my clients. I could've killed him."

The following summer I didn't see Cindy because I was away. When I came back in the fall with my sorry looking set of split nails and overgrown cuticles, I started with my usual, "So what's new in your life?"

She smiled and said, "I got married in July."

"You're kidding. How great! Who's the lucky guy?"

"Victor."

"You met another Victor?" I asked.

"No, the same Victor."

Whoa, Cindy! I thought. I knew I had to proceed very gingerly here. "I thought you said you were always fighting."

Cindy laughed and said, "Yeah, I couldn't take him as a friend. As a lover, that's a different story."

If my hands weren't soaking in her bowl of soapy water, I would have scratched my head in confusion. However, after having read the multitude of studies on male-female relationships, it starts to make more sense to me.

One of the reasons there are fewer male-female platonic relationships than same-sex friendships is because the *hierarchal* male nature comes up against the *solidarity* striving female nature and causes a clash.[61] Men and women view relationships and life in a different way (so what else is new?) and, in love relationships, this can be exciting. Also, in romances, other factors keep the boat afloat.

Another reason is, of course, men's and women's friendship styles are very different. It is common knowledge that men bond by doing things together, women bond by talking. It's hard for a woman to imagine having a close friend, male or female, who didn't bare his or her soul. But a man being asked to bare his soul is tantamount to a woman being commanded to bare her bottom. He'd consider it tantamount to rape if you insisted!

Likewise, how many times do you see a group of women bonding at a baseball game or wrestling match, unaccompanied by males, yelling "Kill the ump?"

I figured now that they were married, Cindy and Victor wouldn't fight so much. But still, she talks about the Victor versus Cindy skirmishes. Additionally they have the challenge of growing the business together and are constantly fighting about which way is best.

They have been married for four years now, so I just had to ask her, "Cindy what keeps you two together, if you're always fighting?"

"Well, it's not *always*," she said with a little smile on her face. "What keeps us together. I guess it's the sex—every night, sometimes twice a night."

"Sex, after four years is still going strong?" I asked (with renewed respect for Victor!).

"Yeah, we fight like a rattlesnake and a cat." She looked up with a big smile and made a clawing movement with her hands. "I keep my nails filed nice and sharp now. They come in pretty handy. Then, about the time I draw blood, we know it's time to make up, and we make fantastic love."

You're the world's expert on what turns you on.

40 What About Turning a Friend into a Lover?

An oft-asked question in my seminars is, "Can you turn a platonic friend into a lover?"

"I haven't run into any studies on this," I tell participants, "but my friend Annie did it. And whether it was accidental or on purpose, I'll never know. And she'll never tell."

Annie is a beautiful, brilliant, and accomplished woman who lives in California. We were introduced about six years ago by her uncle whose company I do various audio projects for. He had planned a small luncheon party, and I was to ride to the restaurant with Annie.

By the time we got there, in typical female style, we knew each other's life story (the ride was twenty minutes), and we were fast friends. One of our big bonds was that Annie also had a Platonic Male Roommate, a PMR named Tim.

"Would either of you prefer not to be so *platonic?*" I asked her.

"Oh, no," she assured me. "It works well this way." I detected a trace of a faraway look in her eyes as she answered, but I didn't know Annie well enough to press.

I've now seen Annie about four times, once each year when I visit her uncle's company. Nothing changes except Annie's title and the ever-growing size of her office. I always ask about Tim. Still roommates, still platonic, and still a sweet smile on Annie's face whenever she talks about him.

My last visit was just a few months ago. This time Annie's reaction was very different when I asked about Tim. She stood up from her big mahogany desk, closed her office door, and said, "I moved out."

"Oh, no, I'm sorry. You were such good friends."

"No, it's good news," she said. "We're engaged!"

"You are what? Tell me, what happened?"

Those of you who saw the 1983 movie can probably guess. Do you remember when Shirley MacLaine and Jack Nicholson, platonic next-door neighbors, got rip roaring drunk one night, danced in the ocean, and wound up in bed together. They had succeeded in holding on to their nightcaps, but didn't do so well with their nightclothes.

Well, it wasn't quite that raucous with Annie and Tim who are both teetotalers. But one tiny drink at a holiday party had its effect, and the next morning they could no longer call themselves *platonic* roommates.

What happened next? Annie moved out. Tim went crazy missing her. He invited her on a ski vacation in Austria, separate rooms of course. And in a charming little restaurant in the Alps, he got down on one knee, brought out a beautiful engagement ring, and proposed.

Important note: I am not—I repeat *not*—advocating battling like Cindy or tippling like Annie to make him or her to take the platonic out of your friendship. However, there's a reason they say, "The course of true love never did run smooth." As in Cindy and Victor's case a touch of inflammatory action can fuel the flames of passion. And in Annie and Tim's case, if you have very strict morals, a little libation can mean liberation.

41 Cupid's Last Words

So, Cupid, what's the last word on keeping it hot? Well, first the *good* news. Yes, you can keep the passionate kind of erotic love going. Now the *bad* news. The three ways to do it are:

1. Be constantly faced with adversity (like Cindy and Victor growing the business together and fighting with each other).
2. Have the relationship forever threatened and be in fear of losing your partner (like Tim's fear of losing Annie, and Annie probably wondering if her *moving out* gambit would work).
3. Be separated most of the time.

Concerning one and two above, there is hardly a love story, play, or movie that doesn't portray lovers whose relationship or lives are not threatened. It's the stuff that love feeds on. In fact many studies have shown the direct relationship between danger and sexual passion. Who hasn't had the old excitement of getting caught fantasy?

One study called "Some Evidence for Heightened Sexual Attraction Under Conditions of High Anxiety" demonstrated the linkage.[62] In fact, since the beginning of recorded time, people have sensed that danger and hot love go hand in hand. Publius Syrus said, "The anger of lovers renews the strength of love." (Who? I don't know who he is either. But he sounds pretty Roman to me and he's quoted a lot in dusty old books.)

Concerning number one, being separated, everyone agrees, "Absence makes the heart grow fonder." This is true—for a while. Then you get so fed up with being alone that you look for some consolation. Often consolation turns to adulation of the consoler. And that spells tribulation for the absentee lover.

In summation, as the trial attorneys say to the jury, you must decide the case. If the loneliness of separation or the fear of losing your lover or your life is worth it, OK. But, that's a pretty steep price. I'd vote thumbs down on the constant PEA urge and go for that other kind of endorphin-based forever love.

Can You Have the Peaceful Forever Kind of Love Right off the Bat?

It depends. A relationship can begin with the more endorphin kind of love when, due to age or other factors, sex has taken a backseat. It is very common between much older couples who are marrying more for companionship than sex. However, younger couples usually need the PEA to kick start their relationship.

An old college friend of mine, Maria, lived with her boyfriend for six years. She said that the minute they met on a tennis court, they felt like old friends. They were perfectly matched in tennis and in the game of life as well. Sometimes I would double-date with them, and I saw how beautifully she and Michael got along.

Maria once told me, "I'm so grateful that Michael is such a nice guy. He's one of those rare men you can talk to. And he actually listens! I always feel like my opinion counts with Michael."

In fact, if there were a nationwide million dollar prize contest for the most compatible couple in America but it cost $100 to submit a couple, I'd have no hesitation about submitting the

♡ MORE MAGNETIC ATTRACTION!

Six massive studies were conducted to find the answer to why people stay together. It may not sound like as much fun as getting drunk and dancing together in the ocean, but for better or for worse, here they are. The happiest married folks are:

1. The ones who believe in the institution of marriage, either as a social or religious force in their lives.
2. The ones who also have a touch of fear of the emotional, financial, and social costs of calling it quits.
3. Above all, they have a devotion and deep respect for the one whom they have chosen as a life partner.

The hot sexy part? *Enjoy it while it lasts!*

M&Ms. (That was their nickname with all their friends.) Whenever any of our friends were giving a party, they'd put the M&Ms on the top of the list because they were so pleasant.

Well, here we go. Astonishment time again. I called to invite the M&Ms to dinner one evening and discovered they were separate Ms now. I was as surprised as you'd be going into a store and asking for M&M's candies and discovering that they were selling the Ms separately now—the centers in one bag, and the chocolate covering in the other.

Maria told me she broke up with Michael because, she said, "We were more like roommates than lovers. Oh sure," she said, "we had sex, but it was like having sex with your brother. It was a warm and comfortable relationship, but never sizzling hot." And that's what Maria craved.

What's Cupid's Secret? What Really Keeps Couples Together?

Powerful stuff, that PEA. So can love exist without it? Yes, the permanent more serious kind of love can, and usually does, last a lifetime. That love incorporates love, not only of each other, but love of some principles of love.

♀♂

CLAUSE #33:

I Won't Toss the Person with the PEA

I do understand that when our wild, wet, wiggly, all-night making love seems to be history, that won't mean our love is. It is with that in mind, I will continue reading to learn how to capture or recapture my life-long love.

---

42 Mirror, Mirror, Find Me a Mate

Now, if you are not currently in a relationship, and masochistically decide you'd like to trade in some of your loneliness for the lunacy of love, this clause will astronomically increase your chances of making someone fall in love with you. It invokes what science tells us about why our hormones dance a jig on our backbone and our knees go to jelly when we look at one person and not another.

Without getting too technical, the organization of neurons in our brain from birth through our difficult teen years is determined by what we see, hear, touch, smell, and feel. That interplay of neurons constitutes our subjective reality. Within that maze, there are patterns associated with the opposite sex. When little girls see Daddy or some other male family figure, it forms her definition of *maleness*. When little Jimmy sees Mommy, or Aunt Ellen, or another female family member, his little brain says, "Ooh, female!" Sort of an instinctive "Me Tarzan, you Jane" reaction.

For children who are fortunate enough to be loved by these opposite sex family members, it's very comforting indeed. The pattern gets reinforced by other (usually) opposite-sex individuals in the family such as aunts and uncles. The boy or girl next door can

More Magnetic Attraction!

People Magnets don't carry a ruler around with them at parties and measure the earlobe, middle finger, and distance between the eyes of a potential mate. But let me momentarily push aside my own mission statement on friends, love, and diversity, and simply offer you this proved scientific fact: if you go out with someone who looks like you, they are four times more apt to fall in love with you.

be a secondary source of these images, but the primary one is usually related individuals.

Now, considering that half of these family folks share half our genes, they look a lot like us. And since our attraction patterns get formed early, it begins to make sense that people are attracted to people who look like themselves! (Therapists prefer a fancier term—people who fit our early gestalt image.)

In a fascinating study, researchers found that married couples resembled each other, as expected, in age, ethnic background, religion, socioeconomic status, and political views. But researchers were blown away when, four times higher on the scale, were similarities in appearance right down to length of earlobes, lung volumes, circumferences of wrists and ankles, distances between eyes, and even length of middle fingers.[63] In other words, we are preprogrammed, from childhood, for *blam* with the proper stranger.

An interesting postscript to this study. It seems that in societies where there is a very high social stigma on being cuckolded, there is a higher frequency of look-alike mating. The men choose women who look like them so that it will leave absolutely, positively, definitely no doubt in anyone's mind from whom their offspring sprang!

CLAUSE #34: LOOK FOR A LOOK-ALIKE ♀♂

If I'm desperately desiring someone to fall in love with me, I will seek someone who looks just like me.

43 Get Off My Duff

Now, for a more practical approach. How do I get the love juices flowing through someone's veins if this person doesn't have the phenomenonally good fortune to look like me?

Well, at the risk of sounding sarcastic, "You have to meet them." Why do I even have the pluck to put something so obvious in writing? Because it's a minor detail that escapes so many wannabee lovers' attention. Sitting home watching TV or talking with their same-sex friends on the phone, they are constantly complaining, "Why don't I ever meet Mr. or Ms. Right?" Since surely you're not one of those many who assumes dream lover will ooze through the telephone wires or come leaping out of the television screen, let's construct a game plan.

Before continuing to read, please list five outside activities you truly enjoy. By outside, I simply mean outside of your own home. It obviously can be indoor like racquetball, or even in a cave like spelunking. Going to lectures on a subject that interests you counts as well. The only unifying factor of the five must be that each is something that you sincerely enjoy.

1. _____

2. _____

3. _____

4. _____

5. _____

Several months ago I was giving a talk to a singles group and a woman came up to me after the seminar and said she was having a horrific time meeting any *cultured* men. I asked what her definition of cultured was.

"Oh, you know," she said, "someone who likes the finer things in life—opera, art, classical music. A man who enjoys dining at fine restaurants, who knows his wines.

"All the guys I meet are jerks," she complained.

I asked if she belonged to any opera societies.

"No," she responded.

Had she gone to any art galleries lately?

"No."

What about classical concerts?

"Well, no."

"Have you ever sat alone at the bar of a fine restaurant or hotel and had a drink?"

More Magnetic Attraction!

"Sure, I know I should go to events alone to meet people." But, until you sign this clause, you're going to make excuses like being dog tired after work and just wanting to put your dogs up and sleep. Well, if you let those sleeping dogs lie, you'll never get any bites. Get up. Get out. Get loved.

"Uh, no."

"What about some wine tastings?"

"I guess not."

I hope her own series of negative responses gave her the obvious answer. You want to catch trout, you go to the stream. You want to trap bears, you go to the woods. And, if you want to find a cultured man, you go to the places where cultured men go.

The problem I could foresee for this woman was, if she wanted a cultured man who liked *some of the finer things in life* as she described them, she'd have to start experiencing and appreciating them as well. If she didn't, after one date (providing she could wangle that), he would be bored realizing how little they had in common.

Therefore, in the long run it doesn't pay to go somewhere to snare the kind of bear whose interests you won't share. The only way to meet Mr. or Ms. Right is, obviously, to go where the folks with the right stuff for you go.

Take a look at the list of your hobbies and interests that you wrote while you were happy and unsuspecting that you would have to sign the following clause. Once signed, you are committed to attending the event or going to a gathering of like minded people *alone*, a minimum of twice a month—four times if you are seriously seeking love in all the right places. When you go to an event alone, your chances of meeting someone new increase astronomically.

Women, this clause is especially important for you since *similarity of interests* is high on the male wish list. It has been proved that a woman's interests are a hot relationship igniter for a man.[64] Men want women they can have fun with, can go to movies with, hike with, maybe (if he's lucky) even a woman who will go to baseball games with.

♀♂

CLAUSE #35:

WEEKLY OFF-MY-DUFF PROMISE

To meet the type of love I want, I will go to an event that interests me once a week—*alone*. (And that's if it's only a half-hearted hunt.) If I'm really serious about finding love, I'll go twice a week.

44 If You Want to Date, You Must Initiate

Is it sufficient to show up? To attend? To make the scene? To punch the clock? To breeze in? That's where most love seekers stop, thinking they've done their bit to find love. They go to an event with some of their same-sex friends and spend the whole evening shooting the breeze with their buddies. Oh, occasionally, they cast furtive little glances at interesting potential partners (trying to look like they didn't) and then expect the other party to take the initiative.

Do you remember how Johnnie Cochran won the O. J. Simpson case? There are those who say he probably did it with one line alone: "If it doesn't fit, you must acquit."

Here's your line for posterity: *If you want to date, you must initiate*. Once initiated, you must then perform a highly choreographed dance called "The Dance of Intimacy." This is a term coined by a dauntless researcher who spent thousands of hours in his laboratory observing animals' mating rituals.

His laboratory? A singles bar.

His subjects? Human beings.

His observations: Who cast the initial glance, and how. Who made the initial move, and how. Who lost interest, and why. Who left together, and why.

In other words, Dr. Perper took careful note of how they met, how they went off to date, and possibly to eventually mate. Over and over he saw the same pattern.

The Dance of Love

It is absolutely riveting to see videotapes of women giving signals to men and men approaching women to see how far they will get in the "Dance of Intimacy." Sometimes they don't last one song. Other times, they become a couple for the evening and, who knows, perhaps a lifetime.

Once begun, the unspoken dos and don'ts in the "Dance of Intimacy" are so rigid that, if you accidentally step on your partner's toes, you are immediately eliminated. There are lots of folks who are great dancers. They know all the old dances—the cha-cha, the Charleston, the conga, the clog dance, the hoochy koochy—but when it comes to the oldest dance of all, real hoochy koochy, more commonly known as *courtship*, they fall flat on their faces.

We will detail the steps which are as carefully choreographed as the most graceful pas de deux. A woman's smile is often the *curtain cue* that begins the dance. Then the actual body movement begins with our ballet prince taking one step—it must be *adagio* (slow). The ballerina responds with a tiny *pirouette* toward him. If she approves of his *placement* she shows a bit of reverence, such as a smile. This encourages him to do a tiny *divertissement* to make her smile again. If she does, he can proceed a bit more *allegro* (quickly). However, his timing must be impeccable. At this point the ballerina must perform some sort of *en avant* (forward motion) to encourage him. If not, the whole dance collapses and each is left to dance *pas seul* (alone).

Sound complicated? It is. But then would we really want to return to some early American customs? For instance, the Crow Indians of North America did have a more direct approach. The male pursued a female by crawling up to her tent at night, putting just his hand inside and if he was lucky (in other words, if she positioned herself just right) his hand found her genitals. He would stimulate them and, if he did a good job, he could follow his hand into the tent and persuade her to have intercourse.

Today, I think most of us would prefer the *whole person* approach to auditioning each other for love.

Inviting Someone to the Dance of Intimacy

There isn't going to be any love dance if it is not advertised or if no invitations are sent out. Therefore, the woman who wants the dance to begin, must either advertise or send out a private invitation. The latter is far preferable over the former because you get a much better class of men responding.

Advertising (not recommended) is going to a bar wearing either a peek-a-bosom dress or one cut up to see level. A private invitation (highly recommended) is smiling at the gentleman you would like to meet.

I'm sure it's happened to you dozens of times across the proverbial crowded room (or, more likely stuffing quarters in the dryer at the laundromat, or shopping for socks at the mall). You spot that special person and *blam*! He got you. Cupid's arrow is sticking right in your heart. You feel unsteady on your feet. Your palms get wet and your throat gets dry. Your mind races for a way to make the approach. While trying to get up the courage, you are reduced to lurking around and furtively looking at the man or woman who you know is destined to be your mate.

It happened to me just last week. There was an adorable man buying socks in the men's hosiery section of the department store. Did I do anything about it?

No (I'm still kicking myself).

Why not? Well my thought process went something like this . . . "Uh, he looks busy. After all, he's making the monumental decision of which socks to buy. Bet his feet are cute too. Wish I could see his left hand, ring finger but it's inside the socks. Oh he's probably married anyway. Besides, what would I say? 'Excuse me, but I think the brown socks would go best with your skin coloring?'"

I finally settle on this courageous and clever comment, "Excuse me, do you know where the men's shirts are?" But, before I took a step, he had purchased his socks and was on the way down the escalator. Bye-bye love.

For the rest of the afternoon my fantasies ran rampant. I saw myself in soft focus, gracefully lifting the most luxurious pair of brown socks on the table, running them sensuously against my cheek, and, looking up at him through my lashes, saying seductively, "Ooooh, try these. They're sooo soft."

He, immediately captivated by my beauty, my perception, my . . . Oh, cut it out Leil! It's just another possible love who got away. And all because I didn't initiate.

If you want to date, you must initiate.

Women, do not be embarrassed about making this first move, i.e., smiling. Your smile is helping to populate the universe. In fact, the earth would have only one-third the number of mammals, marsupials, reptiles, birds, fish, primates, *and* humans if it were not for the female initiation of courtship.

Even though two-thirds of all liaisons are initiated by the woman, I promise you less than 10 percent of the men realize it. Women, you may be infuriated when the man who works in your office actually thinks one of your good ideas was his and tries to take credit for it, but there is a good side to this. In love, no

MORE MAGNETIC ATTRACTION!

Thousands of variations on this scenario are happening at this moment all over the world. The mating game, aborted in its incipient stages. Love with a proper stranger seldom gets beyond the looking stage because we are all reduced to shy children when we spot a potential love. Women, in all the animal kingdom, we are preordained to initiate encounters with the male of our species. Go for it!

matter how blatant your approach is, the male will also think the idea of meeting you was his and he will claim credit for it.

Sisters, take my word for it. You are many, many times more apt to meet the man of your dreams if you can master the simple smile. It's all a matter of attitude. If you happen to be at the prototypical meeting spa for men and women, a pub, don't think of it as smiling at a man in a bar. Rather think of your smile as sending this message:

> "With this smile, I hereby present my compliments to you, and will feel much pleasure if you should choose to grace me with your company at this moment on the stool next to mine. I regret that decorum dictates that after I have delivered this favor of my smile, my modesty decrees I must demur and not allow my eyes the pleasure of continuing to remain on your person. It is my sincere wish, however, that you have understood my intent, and you will permit us the pleasure that I know that we shall both experience in each other's company." Or, in other words, "Hi, c'mon over!"

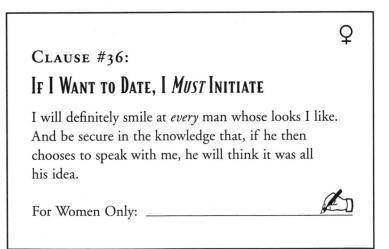

♀

CLAUSE #36:

IF I WANT TO DATE, I *MUST* INITIATE

I will definitely smile at *every* man whose looks I like. And be secure in the knowledge that, if he then chooses to speak with me, he will think it was all his idea.

For Women Only: _____

45 Don't Think Lines, Think Lyrics

Because I'm constantly on the road, I dine alone in hundreds of restaurants around the country. And, being a shameless people watcher, I'd like to offer my own observations. They are, I discovered, thoroughly in accord with the sobering research conducted in bars by the dauntless researcher Dr. Timothy Perper.

Dr. Perper received a two-year grant from the Harry Frank Guggenheim Foundation to hang around singles bars and observe. (Nice gig if you can get it!) Regrettably, I had to pay for my own drinks (or let one of my unsuspecting subjects pick up the tab) if I decided to partake as a subject in my study.

Dr. Perper postulates and proves: "The response of the woman must mirror almost precisely in energy level the approach of the male, or else the meeting usually aborts before it ever has a chance to take off."[65]

Often I would have to sit at the restaurant's bar while waiting for my table, and occasionally someone sitting on the next stool would make contact. Whenever the gentleman said, "Hello," "Howdy," or "How ya doin'" and I responded with equal (not more, not less) warmth, things seemed to progress well. If my reciprocal greeting was less warm (as often was the case if his opening salvo was "How ya doin'?") he would soon retreat. If my

> ## ♥ More Magnetic Attraction!
>
> Women, think music, not words. Remember the pitch pipe your music teacher used? When the gentleman first speaks to you, match *precisely* the amount of energy and enthusiasm in his voice. Too little, you lose him. Too much, you spook him.

reciprocal greeting were much more enthusiastic than his, he was usually the one to stop talking. I realized, after reading Perper's research, he was probably thinking, "A pushy chick?" or "Hmm, desperate, I better run."

Now, if his opening salvo was not super friendly and warm . . . let us say his personality was more reserved and he opened with, say, "Hello, er, would it disturb you if I sat here next to you?" it was best if my response matched his politeness. The enthusiasm and the melody of our voices are crucial if we want to fan the flames of any encounter.

For this gentlemen, the best response would be an equally gracious, "Not at all," or "My pleasure."

Rule # 1 for Women, match *precisely* the enthusiasm, warmth, and energy of the gentleman's greeting. Dr. Perper also observed that, once two people have fallen into conversation, each subsequent step must be an advance of sorts, not a falling back. Or if a backward step is taken, it must be quickly compensated for by two in advance. In other words, there has to be a logical progression toward *coupling*. The steps can be verbal or nonverbal.

For example, *he* comes up to the bar where *she* is sitting.

He: (Turning toward her, he immediately asks, a tad nervously,) "Hi, mind if I buy you a drink?"

She: (A little startled because he sat down on the next stool and immediately asked her the question, she turns just her head toward him and thinks, "Hmm, I do like his looks but, if I let him buy me a drink, I'll have to talk to him the whole time I'm drinking it, and he might turn out to be a jerk. I'll stall it just a little and find out.") "Oh, no thanks, I haven't finished this one."

He: (Thinks she doesn't like him.) "Oh, well (embarrassed smile), if you get thirsty you know where to find me!" (Gets off stool and walks away.)

She: (Thinks, "Wait a minute, he seems kind of sweet. I wish he wouldn't go away.")

But now it's too late.

What went wrong? Who was at fault?

They both were. He was at fault because his sense of timing was off. He should have waited until she had seen him and observed a little of his behavior before making her decide about the drink. She was at fault as well because, she did not meet his enthusiasm with equal energy.

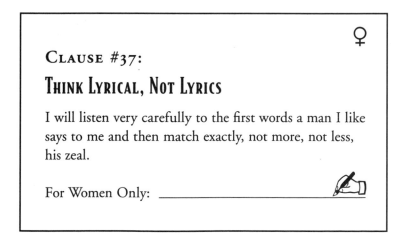

♀

CLAUSE #37:

THINK LYRICAL, NOT LYRICS

I will listen very carefully to the first words a man I like says to me and then match exactly, not more, not less, his zeal.

For Women Only: _____

46 Men "Pick Her Up," Gentlemen "Make Her Acquaintance"

It is a delicate art form these days to make a woman's acquaintance without the benefit of a third-party introduction. First let's talk about the rudiments, and then we'll graduate into more advanced techniques.

Whether you are a Beginner, Intermediate, or Advanced, your approach begins with eye contact. (Note: women do *not* like you to call them "girls"—unless they are over forty in which case it is a compliment.) Here's how to use those grenades over your nose to captivate the women.

Positioning is extremely important. When you first spot the woman you would like to meet, jockey yourself into position so you are in her *direct line of sight*. Then, keep a gentle but fixed gaze on her. Soon she will "feel" your eyes and look up at you. At this point, you give a respectful small nod accompanied by a smile.

She will, naturally, look away. It is part of the courtship rite for women the world over. (Even female rabbits do it and you know what they say about rabbits.) However, you can judge by the *way* she looks away whether she likes you or not. Here is the Aversion/Assertion eye-contact test which I have found to be 100 percent accurate. She first averts her eyes, and, if she looks back within 45 seconds, she is asserting her interest in you.

It is a tad more complicated, however, because you must observe how she looks away. It is a true barometer to her feelings.

She likes you if . . . she looks down toward the floor and away, sweeping the floor as it were with her eyes. The woman who looks away in this fashion probably welcomes your approach. Sometimes a tiny suppressed smile accompanies this downward look. All the better.

She's not sure she likes you if . . . she looks away, horizontally on a flat plain, as in sweeping the walls. This means her internal jury on you is still out. We don't have the verdict yet.

She probably doesn't like you if . . . she looks toward the ceiling and away (in essence rolling her eyes). If she does that, the following test is hardly worth the effort. Other possibilities are, of course, that she finds you attractive but she has a husband or boyfriend and is discouraging you.

Now, presuming she has looked away either horizontally or down, quickly check the second hand on your watch. You are measuring the time it takes her to look up again. If she looks at you within the next 45 seconds, she wants you to make the approach. This is as good as an engraved invitation reading, "You are cordially invited to come talk to me."

Step One: You give her a second smile.

Step Two: Now you walk toward her and stand close enough to talk, but not too close. Keep a respectful distance, yet one that permits easy conversing. The precise distance will vary depending on the room size, the crowd, the situation, and certain other variables.

At this point, you can test her interest again by her body movements. Does she partially or fully turn away? (Bad and very bad signs.) Does she stay in the same position? (Jury is still out.) Does she turn partially or fully toward you? (Good and very good signs.)

Step Three: Now you say something to her which is neutral and courteous, but not personal. If you're at a private party, you can ask how she knows the host. If you're at the theater, you can ask her how she is enjoying the play. Try to ask what is called an "open-ended" question—one that she cannot answer in ten words or less.

You may remember in Part Two, I mentioned someone's first impression of you is 50 percent visual, just what he or she sees; 30 percent auditory, just the sound of your voice; and only 20 percent your actual words.

For that reason pay special attention to something which you are not used to being aware of—the sound of your voice. Women are far more sensitive to this than you. What kind of voices do they prefer? One study called "Voice and Interpersonal Attraction" said that women prefer a voice which is "bright, low timbre, good variety, but not a large range of vocal pitch." In other words, expressive, but not all over the field. Obviously, you don't want to make your voice appreciably different from what it is. But think mellifluous, think warm, think confident. Think "I like you. I'm interested in you—as a person."[66]

At this point, if your appearance passed muster, and if your sound was sufficiently lyrical, and your words were suitably mannerly—in other words if you have completed the three steps correctly—all augurs well. Now is the time to begin comfortably conversing with her. Say the same things to her as you would to anyone whom you would like as a friend, again trying to avoid too many personal questions. During this conversation you can keep your eyes open and judge some of her body language to gauge how you're doing.

♂

CLAUSE #38:

MY THREE-STEP STRATEGY CLAUSE

Whenever I want to meet a woman I haven't been introduced to, I will follow the three-step strategy outlined above and pay special attention to the sound of my voice.

For Men Only: _____

47 The Failure Fallback Plan

Now suppose you make the approach and, alas, she or he rejects you. To take the stinger out of this zinger, gentlemen, and ladies too, I recommend you have a few foxy little face-savers in your pocket. You will find the approach much easier if you have a quick and cool complimentary comment to cover yourself in the unlikely event you are rebuffed.

For example, if she says, "Sorry, I have a boyfriend." You respond with "He's a lucky man."

She says, "I'm not in the mood to talk now." You respond with, "That's my great loss."

He makes it evident that he doesn't welcome your approach. You say, "Please consider it a compliment."

She turns away from you. You respond by saying nicely, "Whoops, I forgot. Let me go take off my invisible cloak and I'll return when you can see me."

She laughs in your face. You tell her, "You have a beautiful laugh."

She moans. You respond by saying nicely, "I only make the most beautiful women ill."

MORE MAGNETIC ATTRACTION!

When you are armed with a compliment or a respectfully funny line, you'll have more courage to make the move on a proper stranger. A really foxy face-saver, skillfully delivered, often turns an early *no* into an eventual *yes*.

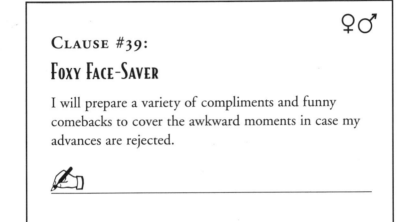

CLAUSE #39:

FOXY FACE-SAVER

I will prepare a variety of compliments and funny comebacks to cover the awkward moments in case my advances are rejected.

48 Creative Courting

Of course, when the competition is rougher, the competitors get tougher, and you need to be a bit more creative in your technique. Let me tell you about one of the most impressive feats of winning the fairest damsel's heart I've witnessed. Then we'll discuss the underlying principle and how you can use it.

You don't have to be James Bond to pull this one off. All you need is imagination and an understanding of beautiful and ambitious womens' hot buttons.

My friend Phil and I were at a party some years ago which, from the looks of it, was definitely stacked against him in the "finding love" department. Phil didn't know anyone there because most of us were members of the same health club. The ratio of men to women was two to one, and the men who were there looked like they'd just stepped off the pages of *Men's Fitness* magazine. Phil to this day has no idea what the inside of a health club looks like. He's more of an *Atlantic Monthly* kinda guy.

I could tell that Phil was bored with the current discussion. Five or six people in our part of the room were passionately sharing their favorite recipes using wheat germ, soybeans, and buckwheat flour. (Phil's favorite foods are pork chops and mashed potatoes with lots of butter.) He turned a little green when a man with Arnold's biceps and a "Baywatch" beach boy's abs started bragging about his daily brewer's yeast and acidophilus milkshake.

Just then the doorbell rang. The host of the party opened the door, and there stood . . . nothing short of a goddess who was gracing the earth with her presence. She was 5'9", with blindingly shiny blonde hair to her waist, and big blue eyes with lashes so long they'd fan flies away.

All heads turned. No highway crash ever rivaled the amount of rubbernecking that swept the party. The electricity she generated was almost lethal as the men's eyes widened in excitement and the women's narrowed into green slits of jealousy.

Much to the delight of the males and the dismay of the females in our group, the host introduced Alexis to us first. She joined in and the conversation gradually drifted from nutrients, protein, and carbs to what all the men were interested in—Alexis. Where was she from? How long had she been living in New York? What did she do? And, of course, there were many hints aimed at finding out if she had a steady boyfriend so the men could know if they could start getting their hopes up. So far Phil had not said a word.

Alexis's answers came smilingly and easily with that California girl charm. Lexi, her nickname, was from San Clemente, California, and she had been living here for about five years with a girlfriend in Greenwich Village. She was an actress and had performed in a number of small theaters, the largest being The Public Theatre in New York. She had gotten a role there soon after she came to New York, and yes, between the lines, she was available.

Now gentlemen, given this information, what would you have done to stand out and capture Lady Lexi's interest? Here's a hint. You have your laptop in your briefcase in the closet.

You may have guessed it. Phil, in full realization that the cards were stacked against him excused himself saying he had to make a phone call. When he came back fifteen minutes later, nature was taking its inevitable course. Most of the women had drifted away, and the throng of men around Alexis was growing.

Phil patiently awaited his chance. Instead of pouncing, he waited for a lull in the conversation and then casually asked Alexis, "Incidentally, how was it working with Joe Papp?"

Alexis's head swung around noticing Phil for the first time. "Uh, you know Joe Papp," she asked.

"No," Phil replied honestly, "but I know people who have worked with him, and I've heard he's, well, not terribly insightful about the theatrical craft. A lot of performers really don't like him. But, of course he is unquestionably one of the most dynamic forces in American theater in the last fifty years. What do you say?"

"Oh, yes," Alexis said cooingly. Phil's insights had interested Alexis. He gradually let the discussion flow naturally from Papp's "raging bull" personality to wondering what Al Pacino, Meryl Streep, Kevin Kline, and Denzel Washington—all of whom have worked with Papp—would say about him.

Soon Phil and Alexis had jockeyed themselves in a side-by-side position. The other men, not getting a word in, soon began to smell defeat and started drifting away. Alexis and Phil then took a walk over to the bar together to refill their drinks. Before the end of the evening, Phil had a date with Alexis to take her to the theater the following week.

Now, do you think it was just accidental that Phil knew all about Papp? Of course not. He knew nothing about Papp, but *the Web* knows everything. That "phone call" Phil had to make was

❤ More Magnetic Attraction!

You've heard the phrase, "I can't go, I haven't a thing to wear." It should be, "I can't go, I haven't a thing to say." People Magnets nibble morsels of information on any subject in the world right off the Web so their tongues will be well adorned for every occasion.

to log on and run a quick search on "The Public Theatre" which turned up "Joe Papp," the founder and director. Phil found everything he needed in one book review on Amazon.com. Although he had enjoyed theatre, I don't even think Phil knew the words *theatrical craft* before that night when he let them roll so comfortably off his tongue into Alexis's beautiful ears.

And, of course, before his date with Lexi, Phil went on-line again and learned all about the play they would be seeing—details about every cast member and the scuttlebutt on the problems the show faced. He started practicing words on me I'd never heard him use before: fringe theater, Great White Way, improv, showcase, equity waiver, strawhat, born in a trunk. He even said, "Break a leg!" to me as I was going off to a speech that week.

Well, Phil certainly did not lack material to engross this fair lady at dinner after the show. Obviously it worked. He and Alexis dated for about six months until Alexis broke up with him because she got a role in a grade B sitcom in California. The one thing Phil had forgotten to research was what to do when your rival isn't a "Baywatch" boy but a role on a wanna-be "Baywatch" show.

♀♂

CLAUSE #40:

HUNT DOWN HOT BUTTONS

I won't leave love to chance. Whenever I know who I want to make a hit with, I'll do my homework ahead of time and click on some information so I'm on the inside track.

 _____

49 ❤ Shhh, He's Ticked Off!

The only time my PMR, Phil, was truly ticked off at me was a few days after Lexi had broken up with him. The previous evening, he had been moping around, and I had resisted saying anything. I figured he'd feel much better after a good night's sleep.

Now it was morning and Phil was at the refrigerator getting his usual breakfast, some Rice Krispies cereal and a glass of orange juice. I asked him what was wrong.

"Oh, nothing," he replied taking the milk and orange juice cartons out of the fridge. I knew precisely what was bothering him and figured it would be helpful to get it off his chest and talk to a friend about Lexi.

"Phil, c'mon, I can tell there's something."

"Leil, I said nothing's bothering me," he said as he poured the orange juice over his cereal. I pretended not to notice until Phil started eating the soggy cereal.

When he spun around to the sink to spit out the orange juice and Rice Soggies, I couldn't help but smile. But Phil wasn't finding anything funny that morning.

"What's bothering me," he shouted, for the first time in the eight years he'd been my roommate, "is your constantly asking me what bothers me."

Constantly? Constantly? I'd only asked him twice.

But, as I learned, for a male, that's two times too many. Phil then disappeared into his bedroom with a fresh bowl of Rice Krispies in one hand and the whole milk carton in the other. "Whew," I thought. I can't believe I did that. I'd read all the good books on gender differences. But what a dummy! I hadn't really drilled it into my head that men hate to be asked what's wrong. They like to think they have everything under control and nothing shows.

I vowed at that moment that the only thing I would ever do around an upset male is let him know I'm there for him if he wants to talk. I'll never make the common mistake of thinking he's just like us women and will feel better getting a problem off his chest.

Sisters, in the hope that you won't either, here is a clause for you to sign.

Now, gentlemen, please do the women of the world a favor. If something is bothering you, try not to be that stereotypical silent, testy, petulant, crabby, acerbic old grouch. Don't stonewall the problem. Go to your wife. Go to your girlfriend. Go to your female business colleague. Women appreciate your seeking their

---

♀

CLAUSE #41:
LET HIM SULK IN SILENCE

I will never again press a male at home or at work to tell me what's bothering him. If he wants to be a silent, testy, petulant, crabby, acerbic old grouch, I'll let him enjoy wallowing in it. The most I'll say is, "I'm here if there's anything you'd like to talk about." I'll say it *once* and then drop it.

For Women Only: _____

More Magnetic Attraction!

Fellas, I know it's hard for you to believe, but you'll gain sensitivity points in a woman's eyes when you share. Especially if you present your problem confidently in a "let me run something past you and get your input" kind of attitude. How often? Once a week is enough.

council or even just sharing a problem with them (except problems with another woman!).

Why is this difficult for guys? Because, a study found, most men, when they have a problem, either feel embarrassed about it or they kid themselves that the problem is controllable.[67] The few who do seek help, are more apt to go to a male friend.

On the surface, going to your amigo, your compadre, your good ol' buddy sounds like good advice. But, unfortunately, it's been proved that another male is the *worst* person to ask for advice. Why?

Because good ol' buddy is probably as ill equipped as you to give or receive emotional support. After all, he suffers an equal handicap in this department—he's been brought up male too. He never learned the necessary skills which are almost second nature to women.[68] Little girls in nursery school encircle one of their classmates who is crying and try to dry her tears. Little boys respectfully ignore one of their own and let the other little boy bawl his head off.

Additionally, your buddy might not take your problem seriously because belittling it preserves your dignity—and that's a higher priority in his mind than actually solving your problem.

Not going to a woman when something is in trouble can actually mar the relationship. A study called "Effects of Gender Role Expectations on the Social Support Process" said that, "Males may develop indirect ways of revealing inner hurts and struggles . . . in order to escape rejection and loss of self-esteem."[69] That means you may do some really scatterbrain, off-the-wall, screwball things to try to suppress the problem. You may think you're being brave. But women will just think you're stubborn. So, please, talk it out with us. (Once in a while, that is.)

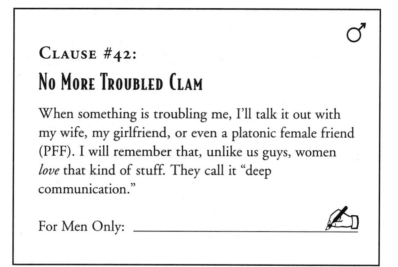

CLAUSE #42:

NO MORE TROUBLED CLAM

When something is troubling me, I'll talk it out with my wife, my girlfriend, or even a platonic female friend (PFF). I will remember that, unlike us guys, women *love* that kind of stuff. They call it "deep communication."

For Men Only: _____

50 Give Me a Strong Shoulder and a Big Ear

Now, gentlemen, a warning. If she is upset about something, don't assume that she wants to be given her space. That's the last thing she wants. She yearns for a strong shoulder and a listening ear—both attached to you. Whether she's the woman who shares your office or your pillow, she welcomes your asking her what's wrong.

For them, it is absolutely no loss of self-esteem to seek help. Just the opposite. "Because females are *expected* to need help in times of stress, men who truly understand women give it to them. They know she both wants and appreciates it."[70]

♂

Clause #43:

What's Wrong, Lambchop?

Conversely, if a woman friend, close colleague, or loved one seems upset, I *will* ask her about it. In fact, she expects me to! If I don't she may think I'm a cad.

For Men Only: _____

---

51 Go Figure!

Now, sisters, it gets a little confusing in the choosing of what to do here because, if he does ask you what's wrong, and you tell him, and he thinks you could have handled it by yourself, there goes his sympathy.

Let me start at the beginning. We were brought up in an atmosphere of nurturing. We played with dolls and gave our little pussycats nice milk in a baby bottle. Then, when the cat didn't like a baby bottle nipple forced down its throat and scratched us to signal displeasure, we would sit on Daddy's lap and bawl our heads off. That's what the researchers call *emotional expression*. By the very fact of being female, we were permitted.

Our brother, on the other hand, when he messed around with the cat and got scratched, was told he was responsible for his own dumb actions. "And furthermore," Dad said, "big boys don't cry."

"So why," we women ask, "when we are adults, doesn't our man act sympathetic like Daddy did? Why, just because he feels we could have handled it, does he get angry? It's not fair!" (What we really want to say is "Why can't you be more like my Daddy?" but we don't dare.)

One Saturday morning several Aprils ago, I had just finished reading a popular book on male-female communications. At the time I was crazy about a boy named Bill, and one of my New Year's resolutions was to get him equally as crazy about me. The book told how much it pleases Martians (men) to help Venusians (women). Being needed reinforces the Martian's masculinity and can sometimes be just the spark needed to ignite love. He feels like he's slaying a dragon for his lady. I pictured Bill dressed in full armor, breastplate tight, steel visor down, lance in hand charging forth to help the poor damsel (me, of course) in distress.

Well, I was in no distress at the time. In fact I had never felt better. Things were great with my work. I'd been able to keep up with my exercises and was feeling good about my body. My love life left a bit to be desired, but I couldn't complain to Bill about that because I was hoping he'd play a big role there. So I "dug deep down to the very bottom of my soul," as they sing in *A Chorus Line* and tried to come up with a problem.

Alas, I couldn't find anything that I needed help with. So, wily female that I was, I invented a problem. That morning I had just finished reconciling my bank statement on a computer program called Quicken, and, as usual, it came out perfectly. But, I figured, since Bill considers himself financially savvy, this is where he can really shine. I opened up Quicken and transposed the amounts on a couple of reconciled checks and deleted the interest and finance charges for that month. Then I closed it out again, and of course it didn't reconcile with the bank statement. Like cards in a poker game, I then strewed my canceled checks out on the table, ruffled the neatly folded statement, and laid it on the top as the center-piece representing my frustration. Then I put on an extra coat of mascara and awaited my modern day Lancelot.

When I heard Bill's knock at the door, I gave one last sweep of my arm across the table of canceled checks to put the finishing touch on their random disarray, and I took a peek in the mirror to perfect my best sweet damsel-in-distress expression.

"Leil, what's wrong?" were his first words when he saw my dismayed expression. (So far so good.)

"Oh, Billy. I'm just having a terrible time with my bank statement. Do you suppose you could answer just a couple of teensy questions for me?"

He smiled. (Hooray it was working.)

I proceeded to show him how I'd entered all the income here, all the checks there, and even the cash withdrawals. He took one look at it and said, "Well, for starters, you neglected to add the interest or subtract the service charges."

"Hmm," I remember thinking. "He doesn't sound quite as protective and happy I was led to believe he would be." Well, maybe he was just hiding his deep-rooted satisfaction.

"And then, jeez Leil, you transposed numbers in the amount column on two checks! How could you have done that?" He sounded agitated. "Do you suffer from dyslexia?"

Then he stood up and pointing to the columns said, "Here fix those and I'm sure it'll come out right. I'm going to go down and wait in the car. Come out when you're ready."

"Bill! Bill!" But he was already gone in a mini huff. "Thanks for figuring that out for me," I called out after him.

"If you'd just be more careful, things like that wouldn't happen," he scowled back.

Now I was seething. "You big doof," I wanted to say. "Here I go to all the trouble to fabricate a situation where you can play the role of hero, and you get ticked off at me." I definitely felt he was the guilty party for being angry.

You Be the Judge

If the case went to trial, Bill's attorney would say, "Ladies and gentlemen of the jury, as you can see from the evidence presented here today, Ms. Lowndes's crime against my client was premeditated, and she had ulterior motives. Her actions involved lying, tampering with records, and attempting to cover it up. My client's anger is completely justified."

My attorney's summation to the jury would be, "Ladies and gentlemen of the jury, my esteemed colleague has, indeed, outlined some of the broad strokes in this case. But remember, this is *not* a case about Ms. Lowndes's creation of a falsehood. His client didn't even know at the time of his anger that Leil had fabricated the story. The only question before the court today is, knowing what we do today about gender differences, was Bill's fury justified at her making the mistake?"

Here's where you come in. You have been flown in as an expert witness. You, a specialist in gender differences, know how males and females typically react in certain situations.

After being sworn in, under oath, you affirm that men do indeed generally like to assist a woman they care for with a problem they can solve. You further affirm that Bill's anger is the issue here.

What testimony can you, as a leading expert in the difference between the way a male thinks and a female thinks, give to prove that Bill's anger was justifiable? Or was it? As you tell, under oath, a little known difference between men and women, you can hear a pin drop in the courtroom. The jury is transfixed.

They are dismissed to decide the case. When they return, the foreman says, "Guilty, your honor. In fact you should lock up Leil and throw away the key."

What testimony could you have given about men and women to bring in this unanimous decision? You told them that Leil overlooked a crucial element in the male psyche. As expert witness, you testify that, given his gender conditioning, Bill had every right to get hot under the collar for being asked to help on a problem *that the woman could obviously solve herself.*

Those are the key words that she "could obviously solve herself." A man does not tend to be angry when his aid is sought on a genuinely tough problem or one that involves a quality that he obviously excells in such as physical strength. *The Journal of Personality* reports that men, unlike women, neither expect—nor give—support to anyone who has made an *avoidable* mistake.[71] (Of course they don't want you to mention it when *they're* the ones who have committed the blooper. But they don't expect sympathy either.)

As expert witness you explain to the jury, "Nobody told Bill he was cute when he was a little boy crying because he skinned his knee. From age four up, nobody kissed his boo-boo and put a Band-Aid on it. He had to take it like a man. Little girls, on the other hand, are coddled and cuddled. Mommy dries her little girl's tears and kisses them away.

Sisters, that does not mean you will never again seek a male's assistance with a problem. If the crisis is a bona fide one, he will be pleased and honored you put your trust in him. Mine eyes have seen the coming of countless concealed male smiles when asked to unscrew the cap from a bottle of old nail polish. Or when their help is sought to show the way to get somewhere from a map. Why? Because he knows he's superior in physical strength or map plotting.

But, take him a problem you could have solved yourself, and you have a very different ending. Women, suppose you misplaced the car keys; you forgot to lock the garage door; or you wore pretty little shoes to go out, and now you don't want to walk from the restaurant to the movie because your feet hurt—*big deal*! (I've done them all.) But, unfortunately he does make a big deal out of it.

"How could you have lost the keys, they were right here?"

"You forgot to lock the garage door! Do you know how much my new racing bike cost?"

"I've told you a hundred times, wear sensible shoes!"

Sometimes, instead of lecturing, men will just stand there stoically while you scramble frantically for your keys. ("Why isn't he helping me find them?" you're grumbling under your breath.

♡ MORE MAGNETIC ATTRACTION!

Sisters, it may not be conscious, but he probably expects you to take your punishment like a man too. Don't be upset. Just let him lecture and take it calmly. Affirm that you will change your ways, and then don't hang on to it. Let it slip out of your grasp like a bar of soap. If you don't, he just might let you slip through his fingers.

You're assuming he's thinking, "This brainless twit, she loses everything." Not true. More likely his mind is many miles away on yesterday's football game.) Or he'll let you go out in the middle of the night in your bathrobe to lock the garage door you left unlocked. Or he'll let you walk with him in your bare stockings five blocks from the restaurant to get the car because you wore uncomfortable shoes. You're thinking, "What a brute! Couldn't he, just for once, go lock the garage door even though it's my fault? Couldn't he, for once, be gallant and give my poor sore feet a rest by getting the car himself and then coming to pick me up?"

Unfortunately, males sincerely believe it's better for you to *learn your lesson* like he was forced to do as a kid. I hope I don't sound like I'm betraying my sex when I say, go ahead. Take your punishment like a man. You are learning a lesson, but not in leaving garage doors unlocked or wearing uncomfortable shoes. You're learning a lesson on how to get along with the man in your life and make him love you all the more!

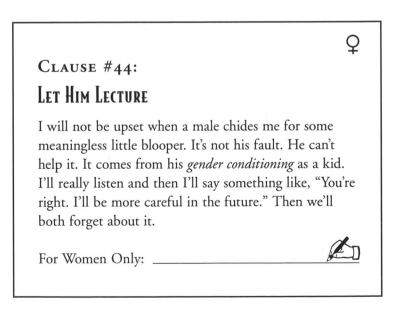

♀

Clause #44:

Let Him Lecture

I will not be upset when a male chides me for some meaningless little blooper. It's not his fault. He can't help it. It comes from his *gender conditioning* as a kid. I'll really listen and then I'll say something like, "You're right. I'll be more careful in the future." Then we'll both forget about it.

For Women Only: _____

52 How Would You Handle This, Dear?

Now, gentlemen, when it comes to asking advice, you too must do your bit to bring harmony and love to the land of male-female relationships. Some of the recent literature on the subject has been too black or white. While it is true that men want to feel needed and women want to be cared for, there is a crossover. A part of the male cries out, "I want to be cared for," and a part of the female yearns to be needed.

Without prejudice, the world now accepts as fact, that women are more sensitive than men when it comes to recognizing the subtleties in relationships. Don't be embarrassed fellas. They've got a few more years of it under their belts than you. Look at any nursery school class. The boys are spread out all over the room with Legos, alphabet blocks, beanie bags, and toy trucks. The little girls are clustered in groups drawing with crayons together, molding clay together, playing with dolls together, braiding each other's hair, and drying each other's tears. If a disagreement arises, they prefer to find a compromise than to battle it out.

A study reported in the journal *Sex Roles* said, "Boys engage in more aggressive and rough-and-tumble play as well as more functional, solitary, dramatic, and exploratory play . . . whereas

> ## ♡More Magnetic Attraction!
>
> The best way to avoid her *Crude Dude* designation and
> win her heart at the same time? Go to her for advice
> with the full recognition that when the good Lord
> assembled women, they were given a bit more DNA of
> the sensitivity type.

girls produce more parallel and constructive play, as well as more
peer conversations."[72]

So, putting these two facts together—women want to feel
needed too, and have been proved *better* at some relationship
issues—what does that suggest to you gentlemen?

If you guessed "ask her advice on certain relationship issues,"
you were right.

It's Not Just for Schmoozing Her

Asking a woman's council is not just a charade to please her. You
can receive some valuable advice and come across as a compas-
sionate leader at the same time. Let's say you are an upper-middle-
management man at a large company, and you must fire someone.
Not a pleasant task. However, I guarantee that one of your female
colleagues will have insights that can make the situation less dis-
tasteful for you *and* the poor chap you have to let go.

At the women's leadership conference I mentioned earlier,
there was one seminar on hiring and firing. Practically every par-
ticipant had, in fact, been faced with the "heartbreaking" task of
having to let someone go.

Twenty people attended, fifteen women, the moderator, and
four men. We went around the room, each narrating how we had
handled firing an employee.

Each of the women in the group had a sensitive suggestion
such as taking the employee to lunch, letting the employee use the
office for another couple of weeks as a job-hunting base, or even

offering to make calls on the employee's behalf for another position. One woman who had to let a good employee go owing to drastic budget cuts gave a small party for her and let her save face by telling everyone she was resigning for a better opportunity.

The four men? To a man, each did it with a sharp clean cut on Friday afternoon. Surprise announcement, "Charlie old buddy, I hate to do this to you but I have to fire you because . . . (the reason). And it's best you have your things out of here before Monday morning." I could tell from the icy expressions on the women's faces that they were feeling not terribly warm toward the men that day.

Gentlemen, you win a woman's respect or love when you handle a situation effectively, but with heart. If these men had consulted with just one of their female colleagues before firing Charlie, they could have picked up a few ideas on how to discharge someone without blasting them.

If you're ever puzzling over how to handle a touchy situation which involves people's feelings or egos, *handling it like a man* could come across as *handling it like a crude brute.*

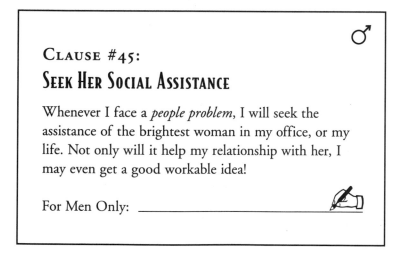

♂

CLAUSE #45:
SEEK HER SOCIAL ASSISTANCE

Whenever I face a *people problem*, I will seek the assistance of the brightest woman in my office, or my life. Not only will it help my relationship with her, I may even get a good workable idea!

For Men Only: _____

53 I Just Want You to Be Happy!

Women, before leaving the lab, we should take yet another peek through the microscope at the neurons circulating in the male brain. It is a well known fact, yet it has failed to make its way into the vortex of the female brain: Men, God bless them, really do feel responsible for our happiness.

If we complain about something, he feels responsible. No matter how much we protest and say, "Oh that's silly," or "Honey, it's not your fault," he feels he is to blame. When you complain that the restaurant wasn't up to snuff, he feels like the chef, the waiter, and busboy all wrapped up in the body of one big failure—him. You didn't like the movie? Suddenly he feels like he's the director, the actor, the lighting man, the sound man, and costume designer all rolled into one big failure—him.

I once went to a terrible movie with a wonderful man. We hit it off immediately, or so I thought. I actually had a fleeting fantasy of sitting by the fireplace with him decades hence with dogs at our feet and children playfully pulling at my knitting and punching at his newspaper.

As we drove to the restaurant for dinner after the show, I shared my cinematic insights with him, worthy I thought of a member of The Academy. The film was set in Elizabethan times, and my keen eye had actually picked up a wristwatch peeking out from the folds of a footman's sleeve. (He would then realize my attention to detail.) I commented on the gaudiness of the castle. (He would, of course, then recognize my design talent for our future home together.)

When we arrived at the restaurant, I was thrilled to discover he was a fellow wine lover. As I peeked over his shoulder at the wine list, I let him know that I knew it was second rate, lest he think I was not a connoisseur of Bacchus' choice beverage. As we sipped our red wine from the flute shaped glasses, I urbanely bemoaned the absence of round goblets. (He would, of course, then realize what a superb hostess I would be.)

Our dinner was mediocre, the service worse. In an effort to let him know how discriminating I was, I let him know. "But who cares?" I exclaimed, batting my mascara-laden lashes. "The company is sublime."

It may have been a no-star film and a one-star restaurant, but it definitely was, in my opinion, a five-star date. We arrived on my doorstep, and I tarried momentarily lest he want to take me in his arms and declare his everlasting love. He let the moment pass, and I, smiling at his desire to impress me with his gentlemanly nature, squeezed his hand in understanding and whispered, "Good night."

As I drifted off into happy dreamland, I half expected the phone to ring. It would be him, telling me what a marvelous time he'd had and asking when he could see me again. And again. And again.

MORE MAGNETIC ATTRACTION!

You are what matters most. Laugh off the gagger movie and dinner that made you gag. Tell her you'll let her pick the next movie and restaurant the two of you go to. (The subtext of that one is "There *will* be a next time." And that, gentlemen, is something a woman who likes you *always* wonders about.)

The phone didn't ring that night, nor the next, nor the next. He never called me again. How was I to know he'd feel like the *@! director of the movie, the chef of the restaurant, and the sommelier? We didn't have all the studies and popular books on gender differences in those days. And I wasn't smart enough to figure out by myself that, even if a male agrees with your critiques, he'll take your disappointment personally.

Gentlemen, what should you do in the case of a rotten movie and a rancid meal at the locale of your choice? Well, first of all, try to rid yourself of those decades of gender conditioning that make you feel responsible. Realize that, nine chances out of ten, contrary to everything you've ever been taught, she does *not* blame you. Same nine out of ten, she accepted the date because she wanted to be with you, not because she wanted to see one of the ten worst movies of the year followed by a trailer for a snuff film and then the Octopus Tartare at the new restaurant with the lousy wine list. Additionally, if she's savvy about gender stereotypes, she'll be worried that you may feel responsible (which you foolishly do) and not want to see her again because of it. So reassure her.

♀

Clause #46:

"You Make Me Sooo Happy"

I will remember that whatever emotion I express, men will feel responsible—and if he can't *fix it*, he feels like a failure. Therefore I will think twice, no thrice, before ever, ever, ever complaining around a man. I'll save that for my girlfriends who will understand we're just hanging out a little disapproval to let it dry.

For Women Only: _____

Of course she'd be happier if the flick had been a blockbuster and the restaurant not so lackluster, but that's minor.

Now here's the important part, dig down deep into your soul, and try to come up with a creative compliment—the more poetic the better. Women love words.

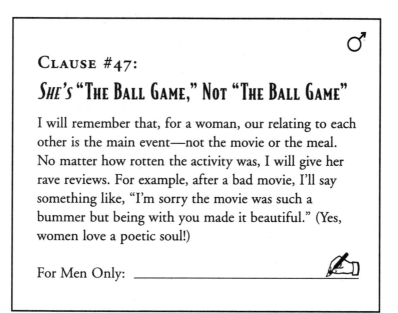

CLAUSE #47:

SHE'S "THE BALL GAME," NOT "THE BALL GAME"

I will remember that, for a woman, our relating to each other is the main event—not the movie or the meal. No matter how rotten the activity was, I will give her rave reviews. For example, after a bad movie, I'll say something like, "I'm sorry the movie was such a bummer but being with you made it beautiful." (Yes, women love a poetic soul!)

For Men Only: _____

54 Hyperbole as Aphrodisiac

Gentlemen, the exaggerated and poetic compliment is not just for the joy of the receiver. Men who have mastered the art form are irresistible to women. Why is it you think that Italian men are considered so sexy? Is it their tall, dark, and handsome looks? First of all, on the average, Italian men are shorter than American men. Dark? Most are, but dark is not the preferred coloring. Handsome? No more or less handsome than American men.

Is it because they are in better in bed? Not according to one of my female friends who has enjoyed both foreign and domestic hanky-panky.

Then why is it that women swoon over Italian men?

I found out in an unfortunate way. All of the waiters on the ship where I was cruise director were Italian. My dinner table was a large one near the center of the dining room, and I always made it a point to invite single people who were traveling alone to join me for meals.

Each week on the first night of the cruise, the waiter would pretend to almost drop his tray because he was awestruck by the beauty of one of the single women at my table.

"Ohh, signorina, and for you? What may I bring you this evening? I am honored to serve such a beautiful woman." Usually that's all it took. My female passenger would be a goner. In the entire season, only one woman saw through it. "Oh, gimme a break," she moaned. So, the next night, the waiter moved on to another of my passengers. The waiter always followed up his *discovery act* with a question for me. "Signorina Leil, where did you find such a bellissima donna on this ship?" (I was tempted to say, "Cut the flap. You know you choose one every cruise.") He would make it quite clear by his allusion to her that if she didn't understand bellissima donna meant "beautiful woman" by the beginning of the meal, she sure did by the end. For each thing she ordered he'd say, "benissimo," which means excellent choice. Often the waiter and the busboy would fall into a mock scuffle on who was going to refill bellissima donna's water glass. If she happened to drop a napkin or a fork, the waiter would race to pick it up and stay on his knees beside her to talk.

All in all it was pretty disgusting, but boy did it work! I shudder to think how many *bellissima donnas* disembarked at the end of the cruise with torn nighties in their suitcases and sated smiles on their faces. They'd be dreaming of their future life in Italy with Giancarlo, Franco, Roberto, Marco, or Umberto.

The only problem was that Giancarlo, Franco, Roberto, Marco, or Umberto never called them again because they'd be pursuing another *bellissima donna* at my table the following week. And did you ever try to ask for a Giancarlo, Franco, Roberto, Marco, or Umberto on the phone in a ship that had several

♡ MORE MAGNETIC ATTRACTION!

You get the idea. Whether you are telling your new girlfriend she is beautiful, or your wife of fifty years that you love her, choose words that could be said in a poem or set to music. Express your feelings in a lyrical way. No matter how clumsy the result, she will love you for your attempt.

hundred waiters all named Giancarlo, Franco, Roberto, Marco, or Umberto?

More than once, when disembarking myself, I saw two *bellissima donnas* who had been my passengers on different cruises waiting on the dock for the same lover and a Giancarlo, Franco, Roberto, Marco, or Umberto ducking through the crowd to avoid them.

Sad but true. But how can we take this sad tale, gentlemen, and make it a happy one? Very simply. Learn how to compliment your lady love. Chances are you are better looking than most of the dining room Lotharios. You are probably brighter and better educated. And you're for darn sure more ethical when it comes to women. But as a nationality, you have not learned one important lesson. A little poetry in your words of love goes a long way. Rent the Italian movie, *Il Postino*. Read a woman's romance novel. Read the English poets. . . .

"How do I love thee? Let me count the ways . . ."

"My love is like a red red rose . . ."

"Come live with me and be my love,
    and we will all the pleasures prove."

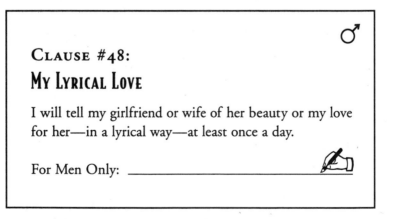

♂

CLAUSE #48:

My Lyrical Love

I will tell my girlfriend or wife of her beauty or my love for her—in a lyrical way—at least once a day.

For Men Only: _____

55 Understanding My Clam

After I watched the Channel 2 news the other evening, there was a program I wanted to see on cable 41. Being in no rush, I decided on a leisurely surf all the way up, channel by channel. (A great excuse to get a quick peek at all those candy-for-the-brain shows that nobody ever admits to actually watching, like "Baywatch" reruns.) When I reached channel 27, I spotted Robert Mitchum, happily snuggled into an armchair reading a magazine, much to the chagrin of a pouting Jane Russell. Being a fan of both late greats, I stopped surfing just long enough to get the gist of the show. Jane was suffering yesteryear's Attention Deficit Syndrome (ADS). Hers was not getting enough of it from husband Robert. The 1951 movie was called *His Kind of Woman* and was, indeed, some kind of awful.

Continuing my leisurely finger voyage, I stopped briefly on a "All in the Family" rerun. Edith Bunker was employing *her* version of feminine wiles to get husband Archie's attention as he sat silently transfixed by the *boob tube*. Finally, Edith blurted out accusatorially, much to Archie's surprise, "You never talk to me anymore." That brought a full can of laughter and applause from the audience. (Such reactions result when we recognize the hilarious truths in our own lives.)

Next in my channel surf, came an "I Love Lucy" rerun. Lucille Ball was whining to on- and off-screen husband Desi Arnez that they don't communicate. She accused him of talking to everyone except her.

"But Lucy, I tell you everything that's on my mind." Laughter and applause. (Refrain: such reactions result when we recognize the hilarious truths in our own lives.) As the episode continued, it became evident that he did tell her everything that he considers important. It's just that, like most males, he doesn't consider his every passing thought important enough to impart. Whereas Lucy, like most women, would have been quite content drifting along on her man's stream of consciousness—whether the stream ended up any place he thought important or not.

I began to pick up a reoccurring theme and I remembered the countless times I've been in the company of a male—whether he was a date at dinner, a PMF at a party, or a male colleague just walking down the street—I always felt we had to make conversation because, if he and I weren't talking, I felt something was wrong. Unless we were sharing ideas, I felt we weren't being compatible.

The Jane Russell character felt the same, Archie Bunker's wife felt the same, and Lucy felt the same. I am sure we are not the only four women in the world who want more communication from the men in our life.

The next day, that was proved to me in a small upstate town where I went for a manicure with Cindy the best nail tech in the country who leads a double life as a town gossip journalist. To her credit, she doesn't reveal names, but Cindy is an entire broadcasting station with a new audience of one every hour on the hour. (She likes it when I tell her I get my international news from the *New York Times*, my national news from the TV, and my local news from her.)

As I sat down and submitted ten chewed and chipped nails for her scrutiny, I opened with my usual original and precisely worded refrain, "So Cindy, what's new?"

She responded with her traditional two word overture (which signals the coming of the latest and juiciest town gossip), "Nothing much."

Now Cindy does not exactly need a clam opener to pry out the latest pearls of local gossip. All it takes is a sentence or two of encouragement. "Oh, come on Cindy, I've been on the road for almost a month. What's everybody talking about?" Everybody, of course, in Cindy's world of nails and hair, meant *women*.

"Oh, it's the same old stuff," she replied. Then she launched into her half-hour program of news and pogrom against the husbands. "They're complaining about the weather and that their husbands are work obsessed and don't talk to them. Especially the younger ones. They're really upset because they say their honeys talked a lot when they were dating. Now they've all turned into clams. . . ."

There I had it—the evidence I needed! From 1950 right on up into the new millennium, women were, and still are, complaining about men's obvious lack of loquaciousness. Cindy and I joked about silver-tongued princes turning into grunting frogs rather than vice versa.

"No, not frogs," she said. "Nowadays brides wake up to their handsome prince and he's turned into, not a frog, but a clam!" The hooting and hollering of all the nail techs and customers within earshot confirmed the verity of her observation. (Refrain: such reactions result when we recognize the hilarious truths in our own lives.)

Who Talks More? Men or Women? Suppose you are on a quiz show. The studio audience holds its breath while the host asks you, "For one million dollars, can you tell us please . . .

Do men talk more than women?

Do women talk more than men?

Or is it about 50/50?" Don't peek!

If you guessed that men talk more, you are now a millionaire. There have been countless studies on verbosity, and not one was able to prove that women spoke more.

So why do women have the erroneous reputation of being terminally chatty? Some speculate the stereotype evolved from men's historical belief that women (like children) should be seen and not heard, so whenever they do speak, some male listeners think it's too much.[73] Others attribute it to the fact that women talk more about people, feelings, and relationships.[74] Because the home is

More Magnetic Attraction!

Your wife/girlfriend/significant other is not as high maintenance as you think. Start using the Minute an Hour tonight and you'll see the difference in her happiness. All of those "mini" first impressions you make each day, add up to an overall impression of a man who cares about the minutia in her life. And that, dear gentlemen, is contentment to a woman. We are not such complicated creatures after all.

more appropriate for these *softer* topics, it often seems like they talk more—because they do, at home. But the men more than made up for it at work. In both *words per day* and amount of time spent talking, men came in first.[75]

Men, on the other hand, prefer topics such as business, money, and sports. Money and business are relevant to their jobs so they really gab it up there. And sports? Well, sports are an important way of male bonding.

Also talking means something different to men. For them, it is a way to call attention to themselves and their ideas—a competing and conquering of sorts. When a man is at work, he's competing for position. When he's with his buddies, he's competing for who's up, who's down. When he's on a date, he's competing to win you. But, at home, happily married or snugly seated with his significant other, he feels no need to compete. The result is contented *silence*.

Clams à la Greque

I have a friend Nicole, a very beautiful young woman whom men swarm around like bees swarm around honey. She is the daughter of one of my clients and, when we met, she unofficially adopted me as "Big Sis." Even though men find Nicole irresistible, she is able to resist most of them. In fact Nicole is quite discriminating and seldom is intimate with any of her suitors. However, Dimitri was a different story.

When she met Dimitri, she knew he was the one. He was very tall, very dark, and very very suave. Dimitri was born in the States, but his father was a Greek shipping magnate and he had traveled all over the world. Additionally, he was an avid reader, so he was very well versed in just about any subject that interested Nicole.

But the best thing about Dimitri, Nicole told me, was that he really knew how to treat a woman. She had been dating him for six months, and he had taken her to two plays, one opera, six movies, one ballet, and countless fine dining restaurants. Every time he came to pick her up for a date, he brought her a beautiful fresh flower. "This guy really knows how to court!" she told me. I felt sure they were on a beautiful winding path which would eventually wind up at the altar.

Whether she was playing hard to get or whether her principles were stronger than her passion, I'll never know, and I didn't probe. But six months into the relationship, she had not yet been intimate with Dimitri.

Then, one Sunday afternoon, Nicole called me in tears. Between sobs she blurted it all out. "I'm afraid it's all over with Dimitri. He's no longer interested in me. I don't think he'll ever call me again."

"Oh, Nicole, I'm so sorry. What happened?"

She confided that last night she had invited him to stay over at her house. She paused dramatically, and then added ". . . all night." I was expected to know what she meant which, of course, was as easy as peeling a banana.

"Oh no, he was terrific," she sobbed. "And I thought I was too," she added (I suppose thinking "Big Sis" would doubt her allure). "So this morning, I asked him if he'd like some breakfast. He said, 'That would be great.' But . . . but . . . but while I was fixing him an omelette, he picked up the newspaper from my doorstep, went into the living room, and started reading!

"If that wasn't enough," she sniffled, "when I served the eggs and sat down for us to eat together, he was still reading! I couldn't believe it.

"I asked him if the eggs were OK, and he smiled and said 'Yes, they're great.' And then he goes back reading. Leil, I couldn't believe it. There I was staring, not at a lover, but at *the backside of a newspaper*. He hates me because of last night. Does he think I'm cheap? Is it because he's Greek?" she asked in desperation. "Is it because when a man gets what he wants, he's no longer interested?"

It sounded as though Dimitri had passed his physical exam with flying colors but left a bit to be desired in the oral department. He should have, of course, understood women better and talked with her warmly over breakfast. But, since he didn't, "Big Sis" had to explain the facts of life to her. No, not the birds and the bees. She had that part down pat. But about clams.

I tried to explain to her that, to many men, talking is to win something—an argument, the respect of a boss or his colleagues, a woman.[76] And, when he is feeling completely comfortable, there is no need to talk. To many men, life is a talk show—and everything he says must be right. But that's work! And when he's with the woman who loves him, he can happily relax, and be quiet.

"Nicole," I said, "Dimitri reading the newspaper at the breakfast table was most probably an indication that he felt completely at ease and relaxed with you."

As I talked, it sounded as though the telephone was in less danger of being short circuited by her tears. I think she began to understand.

Incidentally, her story has a very happy ending. Nicole's name is now Nicole Stephanopolous.

"Hey, that sounds pretty good," I can hear you gentlemen say. "Great, no more of her asking, 'How was your day?' when all I want to do is read the paper. No more of her asking, 'Is something bothering you, honey?' when all I was doing is scratching my head. No more of her saying, 'You never talk to me!' when all I was doing was figuring out a problem from work. And, best of all, no more of her offering, 'Penny for your thoughts!' Hooray! Hooray!"

Not so fast, Brothers. Yes all of the rewards above can be yours. But you have to do your part too. What if I told you that, for a scant fifteen minutes per calendar day, you can make her feel like you rival Romeo. You can make her very happy indeed—both romantically and sexually. (Which, of course, makes you happy sexually.)

Do you agree that the first impression you make on someone new is important? I'm almost sure you do. But the old phrase, "You never have a second chance to make a great first impression" is only half true. Even though you don't have a second chance at the very first impression, you have thousands of second chances at the little first impressions she gets every time you see her. What happens first when you walk into a room or she walks into a room is what stays in her heart for a long time.

Here is the technique to give her the impression that you are not the clam, but a loving and interested friend, significant other, or husband. I call it the "Minute an Hour Treatment." Quite simply, give 100 percent of your attention to your woman for the number of minutes that correlates with the number of hours, up to twenty-four, since you last saw her.

Here are the rules.

The Eight-Minute Treatment: If you and she have been apart for more than eight hours such as at work or on a business trip, devote the *first* eight minutes of your time 100 percent to her. Put down your briefcase, your luggage, your newspaper, and tell her about your day. Ask her about hers. Be sure to work a kiss or an "I love you" into your repertoire.

The Five-Minute Treatment: If you've been apart for a half day or up to five hours, devote the first five or six minutes of your time 100 percent to her. Make small talk. Work a little compliment somewhere into the dialogue.

The Two-Minute Treatment: When you've been apart for just a couple of hours, make sure she has 100 percent of your attention for at least two minutes.

The One-Minute Treatment: And, if you've only been apart for up to an hour, give her at least sixty seconds when you meet.

♀

Clause #49:

My Silent Partner

I will *not* misunderstand that, just because my man isn't talking to me it means he is upset. I'll let him savor the silence and go happily about my business.

For Women Only: _____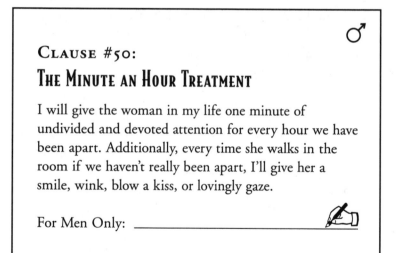

♂

Clause #50:

The Minute an Hour Treatment

I will give the woman in my life one minute of undivided and devoted attention for every hour we have been apart. Additionally, every time she walks in the room if we haven't really been apart, I'll give her a smile, wink, blow a kiss, or lovingly gaze.

For Men Only: _____

PART FIVE

NETWORKING

Recruiting Knights for My Personal Round Table

56 The World's Best Contact Sport

Once You Learn How to Play It

I sincerely hope you never need to suffer, as I did, to be convinced of the need for faithful friends and true love in your life. But if ever something strange flies out of your left field, you want to make sure you're surrounded by a strong team to carry the ball for you until you get back on your feet.

If you are blessed with a close family, you've probably already got a pretty good support system. But sometimes even their love is not enough. Let's say, heaven forbid, a drunk driver hits your car. Because of your severe injury, you must undergo a rare type of surgery. Of course your family will do everything they can to care for you but, unless they are insiders in the medical community, they may not be able to find just the right specialist to make you better than new. (Or the right lawyer who can win a just settlement to pay for the operation!)

In any industry, there are the second-rate practitioners, the standard ones, the stars, and the superstars. The superstars are those who are most knowledgeable. They address their conventions and write articles for their industry publications. The top lawyers and surgeons are on the cutting edge (no pun intended) of their fields, renowned within their professional communities, but relatively unknown outside of it. And only the insiders know who's who.

You might be tempted to say, "Why? If I need a specialist, my doctor knows who to refer me to." "Or, if I need a lawyer who specializes in personal injury, my attorney can refer me." That's not good enough! Their patients or clients (you) are important to them. But more important to them by far are the doctor's or lawyer's family and personal friends.

If you want one of the top men or women on your case, you have to know someone who is not just going to give you the *party line*, or "the HMO doesn't permit me to make recommendations," or "they're all good." You want an insider friend so you can get the real score on these national or international experts.

Local superstars are significant *knights* too. In your hometown or nearby there are bound to be superstar dentists, accountants, bankers, travel agents, veterinarians, insurance experts, firefighters, politicians, headhunters, journalists, auto mechanics, body-repair people, and sales folks—all of whom welcome your business. There are also very approachable superstar cops, politicians, postal employees, firefighters, journalists, and radio/TV media celebrities. These are great knights to have sitting at your Round Table.

57 "Networking?" Did I Hear You Say "Networking"?

Many people abhor the whole idea of networking. I've heard all the excuses.

"Networking is when you become an insincere, groveling sycophant bootlicker to anybody who might be able to help you."

"Networking is pretending you like someone so you can get something out of him."

"I tried networking last Thursday and it didn't work."

"Networking makes my nose too brown."

People suffer two big misconceptions about networking. One, they think it's selfish. Two, they feel uncomfortable mingling and meeting strangers. We're going to *cure* both these conditions.

Because networking has achieved a bad name with some people, I'm giving it a new name. "What's in a word," you ask. "Will just changing its name make it any more palatable?"

Ask pro-choice people about the term *pro-life*. Ask people living *alternative lifestyles* about the word *perversion*. Ask people who support freedom of expression about the word *pornography*. (Please note, I do not imply any judgment on the words above. I merely present them as my case for "What's in a name.")

I'm changing the name *networking* to *Sharing Your Gifts*, or capitalized *Sharing* for short. That's really what networking is all

♡More Magnetic Attraction!

You may still say, "I hate networking." But I'm sure you can't say (and mean) "I hate Sharing my gifts with people I really like." Don't think of *networking* in the old sense of brown-nosing people who can help you. See it as actively seeking people you genuinely like. Then the two of you share your God-given abilities and learned talents with each other so that you are better able to take care of yourself and your loved ones.

about. It's Sharing your talents and gifts with new people you like, and letting them share theirs with you.

Sharing is as much *giving* as getting. Often it's more. Is it work? Yes. It's like exercising by doing sit-ups, lifting weights, or running to take care of your body and strengthen your muscles. Some people enjoy it. Others don't enjoy the actual workout, but they're thrilled with the results.

It's the same with Sharing. Some people love the mingling, the talking, the exchanging of telephone numbers, E-mail addresses, or business cards. For those who don't enjoy the mingling minute-to-minute, think of Sharing as a pleasant workout. It strengthens you to be able to take care of yourself and your loved ones now, and for whatever surprises come in the future.

For example, say you have an aging parent who can no longer live at home. You definitely don't want to put Mom or Dad in an old age home you know nothing about. But if you have Shared with someone knowledgeable, perhaps a geriatric nurse, he or she can suggest who to turn to for home care, or recommend an institution which is a caring and loving environment.

Some of your old friends are moving into your area and have asked you to help them find a home? But you know nothing about rents and prices of houses. You and your friends are in luck if you've already Shared your gifts with a real-estate broker. Due to his or her connection with you, a friend, your broker will give them better service.

Let's say you've done very little travel in your life and now you're taking your first big trip across Europe. You'll have a much more fun, and less expensive trip if you've previously Shared your talents with a travel agent. Because he or she is your friend, you'll get personalized service.

♀♂

CLAUSE #51: SHARING MY GIFTS

I will force myself to go to events and find people with whom to Share my talents for an even more important aspect than my work, and that's my personal life and the well-being of those I love.

✍ _____

---

58 Plan Ahead!

One of the most valued knights sitting at my Round Table is a fellow speaker named Jeff who, selflessly, has done dozens of favors for me. He's recommended me to his clients for speeches and he's *the* man to call whenever I need to get the lowdown on a speaker's bureau or anything else in the *speaker world*.

Some time ago, he called and said his beloved brother and his wife and two kids were coming to New York, and they were dying to see *The Lion King*. At that time *The Lion King* was the hottest ticket in town, and you had to wait almost a year to get tickets even for a Wednesday matinee. And they wanted tickets on Friday night!

Jeff, like practically everyone else in the United States outside of New York City figured, just because I lived in the rotten apple, I had *connections* and could render the impossible. Sure, Jeff.

Well, foolishly, that's precisely what I said, "Sure, Jeff." As I hung up I wondered how in the world I was going to go about getting Jeff's brother, Jeff's wife, and little Amanda and Mitchell tickets to *The Lion King*. I didn't know any big-deal ticket agents. I didn't know any hotshot public relations people who can always wangle seats for their clients. I didn't even know any unscrupulous, slimy ticket scalpers who illegally sold tickets for a scandalous price. I felt terrible because Jeff had Shared his Gifts with me so much. Finally, I was being offered the opportunity to Share back, and I was going to have to let him and his family down.

The only person I knew remotely connected with theater was Pam, an actress. But she, like most performers is *between engagements* 95 percent of the time. And when she was performing, it was mostly in off-, off-, off-, off-Broadway shows. The closest she ever got to Broadway was my office on lower Broadway where she did part-time secretarial work. "Well," I said to myself, "It's worth a shot." But I knew it was a long longshot.

With no expectations whatsoever, I called Pam and explained the situation. She said she'd get back to me. I had hardly put down the phone when she called back and told me she was 99 percent sure she could get them seats on that Friday if they didn't mind not all sitting together.

After I extracted my jaw from the phone mouthpiece, I managed to mumble Jackie Gleason style, "Hmmma, hmmma, hmmma, Pam, how did you manage to do that?"

It turns out she was dating an actor whose day job was selling tickets in the theater where *The Lion King* was playing. He told her they always have people turning in tickets because their trip was canceled or whatever. And instead of selling them to one of the crowd outside the theater—who offered him bribes of everything from money to their firstborn child—he would save the first four tickets that came in for Jeff's kin from Columbus.

Thank heavens for Pam. I lucked out on that one. But I won't always have a friend who is dating someone who works in the ticket office of a hot show. And even if I did, he wouldn't always be the type of guy who can sneak the family of a friend of a friend of his girlfriend to the top of the list. I resolved at that moment to research who gets tickets how, and put that person on my list of people I'd like to Share my gifts with. (You may notice I'm not telling whether I succeeded or not, lest other out of town friends crawl out of the woodwork wanting me to get them tickets.)

Think about what needs might crop up in your life during the next year. Then imagine who can be a solution to those potential problems.

59 The Guide to Sharing Your Gifts

Many networking guides will tell you how to sidle up to the people you want, get their attention, get them to like you, and go for what you want. Instead, let's reverse that. This handbook of Sharing starts with what *you* bring to the table. It is more blessed to give than to receive and all that. (It's also a smarter way to go about this whole thing.)

Think about what qualities, talents, or knowledge you have that would benefit anyone who knew you. Many of your gifts will be outside the job arena. For example, my PMF Phil, a freelance business writer, is not rich. He's not famous. And he's not well connected. But Phil has a multitude of other qualities which make him an excellent knight to have sitting at anyone's Round Table.

Phil is an obsessive computer genius and will not rest easy until he's solved a friend's software problem. In fact, whenever a friend has any kind of computer quandary, he takes it on as his own and tirelessly pursues the answer. Sometimes I picture Phil like a restless golden retriever in a rocket. Shoot him out into cyberspace, and he lands safely back on terra firma with his tail wagging and the information you wanted securely between his teeth.

He also has an excellent legal mind and will inspect every angle of a contract with the care of a guard making the midnight rounds with a flashlight. Then he'll pick out any potentially both-ersome clause like a monkey picks fleas out of his fur and explain it to you.

The list goes on. He never has a bad word to say about any-one, and his loyalty to his friends is unwavering. Qualities like these are priceless today because they're the type money can't buy.

Maybe you are a *Phil* to your friends. You may not have pre-cisely these qualities, but undoubtedly you have many others that make having you as a friend an invaluable gift. One thing is cer-tain. You are a resource for everything you know. And the more you know and learn, the better knight you are.

For some, networking is easier if they think of it as giving rather than receiving. Imagine yourself sitting as one of the 150 proud knights around Arthur's great table. When it comes time for you to be knighted as one of King Arthur's legion, you are going to tell three reasons why someone would want to be your friend.

There are probably fifty reasons so it's going to be hard to nar-row it down to just three. On this list you can put anything— from a quality you have to a special knowledge you possess.

For instance, perhaps you are unfalteringly honest, so anyone who has the pleasure of knowing you could have faith that he or she would always get a candid answer to anything asked. Perhaps you know more about current rock groups than anyone else, so people can benefit from your recommendations about which con-cert tickets to buy. Perhaps you know all about gardening, so you can suggest to your friends what will grow best in their soil.

If you don't come up with three, ask your family or friends what they consider some of your valuable and sharable qualities. Often you have no idea that your natural talents could have such value to your friends.

Networking, It's Kid's Stuff, Too

Christine, a single mom who also works as a dental assistant, was giving a small tea party for a friend of mine who just had a book published. During the tea, Christine's daughters were scurrying around getting everything ready for their exciting afternoon. Their mom had just bought a microwave, and the girls were thrilled that it could actually make popcorn—and you didn't have to put any oil in the pan. They had popped a huge batch and decided to sell it with lemonade out front. They made a sign "Lemonade 25 cents. Popcorn 15 cents" and raced out to the front lawn to open shop.

After an hour or so, Sarah, the oldest, came in stuttering from tears dripping into her mouth. "Mommy, we sold a few lemonades, but nobody's b-b-b-buying our popcorn. And we have t-t-t-tons of it left."

While we were trying to console her explaining that it wasn't her fault, people just don't eat popcorn on a warm day, the phone rang. Christine answered it and I heard her in the kitchen sharing the popcorn story with the caller. Then she was silent for a minute or so. The next thing I heard was, "What a great idea. We'll try it."

Christine returned with a big smile on her face. "Sarah, go get the crayons and some paper. It's going to help you sell your popcorn." Drying her tears with her fists, Sarah scurried off to get the tools. I asked Christine what was up. She said that the call was from a new friend she had met at a National Association of Women in Business networking event. She was an advertising copywriter who was interested in finding a good root canal specialist, so she was calling Christine for a recommendation. When Christine told her about the popcorn fiasco, she suggested different wording on the sign.

Sarah returned holding her crayons and paper out to her mother with a look of total trust that Mommy was going to perform miracles with the multicolored magic wands. And so she did. She took the crayons to the big paper and wrote a few words in big kid-like letters with backward Rs like Toys R Us. She told Sarah and Ashley to go post it on the stand. Sarah asked what it said. Christine just responded, "These are magic words that will make people want to buy popcorn."

She was right! An hour later both girls returned, looking exhausted but happy, and together carried a big empty popcorn bin.

What had the top Madison Avenue copywriter who had worked on campaigns for companies like Neiman Marcus and Cadillac suggested as the popcorn slogan?

"Today only. Free popcorn when you buy one lemonade for 50 cents. Popcorn has no butter, no salt, no calories, no taste."

Everyone walking by who saw the sign stopped, laughed, and, of course had to taste the tasteless popcorn. Even people who were driving by pointed it out, and many stopped to buy lemonade and nibble on the tasteless popcorn.

Just as the advertising copywriter probably would not have guessed that her talents could have helped a dental assistant with two kids, you may not see how your particular talents can help someone else, but I'm sure they can. A knight doesn't always have to fulfill a big need in someone's life. Knights can plug small holes too. But for Christine, a single mom, her daughters' happiness was no small hole.

♀♂

CLAUSE #52:

KNIGHT TIME-SHARING

Seated as one of the 150 proud knights at King Arthur's Round Table, I submit these as my three top gifts:

1. _____

2. _____

3. _____

I will selflessly share my gifts above as my friends' needs arise and accept graciously when they offer me theirs.

✍ _____

---

60 Do You Carry Enough Friend Insurance?

Now, hopefully, you are comfortable with what you can give. It is time to get comfortable knowing what you can get from letting others Share with you. Recently I saw an ad for on-line banking which showed a pile of little plastic bathtub ducks strewn all over the floor and in piles as though shoved into a closet. The caption under the chaotic topsy-turvy mess was "My Life." The next photo showed a nice neat line of ducks, one swimming in procession after the other, not wavering one millimeter from the formation. That caption was "My Finances."

I could have had a similar ad for myself several years ago. One photo would be me all gussied up to give a speech. I'd be dressed in a stylish suit, carefully pressed blouse, freshly shined shoes, carefully coifed hair, and freshly painted fingernails perfectly matching my lipstick. The caption under that one would be "My Career." The caption under the second photo would be "My Car." Here would be a ten-year-old, banged-up bucket of bolts which, much to my chagrin, was constantly in and out of the repair shop.

Why didn't I chuck it and buy a new car? It wasn't that I couldn't afford it. It wasn't that I didn't want a new car. It was just that I didn't know anything about cars, and I didn't know anyone who did! So year after year I kept putting the painful process of buying one off, all the while making sure my triple A card with the extra towing insurance was in the glove compartment.

Then something happened that was, what you call a *wake-up call*. I was driving to a speech at a recreation center. As I drove to the back of the building to park, I noticed two workmen walking toward the building. I parked and, not knowing where the main entrance was, ran to catch up with them. I overheard one say to the other, "Didja see that little piece of s___ that the speaker drove up in?"

That was it! I resolved to get a new car immediately. In the end I know I paid thousands of dollars too much and didn't get the best car I could for the money, but that was the price I paid for not having Friend Insurance in the car department.

I'll never make that mistake again. I also resolved to never be without a knowledgeable contact for every conceivable predicament I might find myself in. I needed to fill my Round Table with car salespeople knights, accountant knights, doctor knights, lawyer knights, auto repair knights, plumber knights—the list goes on for me. And it does for you too.

Why is it a man and a woman are more apt to go out when they meet at a singles function than if they meet in, say, a museum? Because the mind-set at a singles function is love. They are more open to having love walk in. Everyone of the opposite sex they meet is judged as a potential date.

When we get serious about Sharing our Gifts, we will begin to look at everyone we meet as a potential knight. The next time your sister mentions she's going out with a cruise ship captain, squelch your jokes, "Boy, if he ever takes you and all your luggage on a cruise, he'll have to get a bigger ship. Har-har!" Instead, ask to meet him. Your brother is going out with an accountant? Don't ask if she has the usual qualifications for being an accountant— "you know, appallingly dull, unimaginative, timid, spineless, no sense of humor, tedious company, and irrepressibly drab. Har-de-har-har." Instead, ask to meet her.

In your lifetime, you will in all probability buy six cars, have four houses painted, make five moves, buy twelve insurance policies, take four trips abroad, and purchase innumerable major appliances. You'll call a plumber thirty-six times and an electrician sixteen. In addition you will dine at thousands of restaurants, engage half a dozen lawyers, and buy food and use telephone services every day.

To get the best deal in these, you should definitely have a car salesperson, a painter, a plumber, an electrician, a mover, an insurance broker, and a travel agent on your Sharing Gifts list. So you can get the inside track on products and food, you should also seek someone who works at a major appliance store, a grocery store, and the telephone company. These folks can let you know about the best deals ahead of time and, if they're close friends, they might even put the purchase through them so you can take advantage of their employee discount.

When you've filled in every line of the Friend Insurance Policy in Chapter 61 with the name of at least one person you could consider more than a purely professional contact, you'll have a pretty impressive Friend Insurance policy.

♀♂

CLAUSE #53:

KNIGHT RECRUITING CLAUSE

I will be on the constant lookout for people I like who are the best in their particular field, Share my Gifts with them, and go out of my way to become their friend. I will aim to fill in every blank in the Friend Insurance list.

✍ _____

61 One Man's Knight Is Another Man's Nobody

Below the last job you will find a few blank spaces for you to fill in knights who might be important in your particular life. For instance, a skydiving champion or head of the school board might make great knights for you but, since I'm not jumping out of airplanes or sending kids through school, worthless to me. I'd rather have Jeff and all of his speaker's bureau knowledge, which might bore you. Those last lines are your *Just For Me* Knights.

But just as your insurance policy expires if you don't pay the premiums, your friends will *expire* into acquaintances if you don't keep *paying the premiums*. The cost? Very little, considering the benefit. It's an occasional card, an E-mail, a phone call. It's sending them a clipping of something they are interested in. It's sending birthday and holiday cards. Think of each of the following as a log to throw on the fire to keep the friendship warm.

Friendship is caring about the friendship as much as it is deep communication. There was a man and his wife who owned the little gymnasium I used to go to when I lived in France. We never communicated about any deep feelings or philosophies (mainly because I wouldn't be capable of it in French—and his English was worse than my French if that's possible), but the relationship was quite pleasant. Every year, we've exchanged Christmas cards and he occasionally sits down and writes a letter. Yes, the old fashioned way—pen, paper, envelope, stamp, the whole bit.

There were many people I was closer to when I worked in France. But because Alan and Charlotte kept up the contact, I still consider them friends. I've invited them to come visit me, and I know there's always a place for me to stay in the tiny coastal French town of La Boule.

As you look at the following list, you may think "But why would I need a veterinarian? I don't even have a pet." You may not have one, but remember, as a knight, it's one for all and all for one. There's a pretty big chance you've got some dog-owning knights sitting at the table, and one of their dogs is going to get sick as a dog someday and need a vet.

62 My Friend Insurance Policy

Or the Knights at My Round Table

Job	Name of Person I Know
Accountant	_____
Artist	_____
Banker	_____
Car Repairperson	_____
Community Leader	_____
Elected Official	_____
Firefighter	_____
Headhunter	_____
High Ranking Cop	_____
House Painter	_____
Insurance Expert	_____
Lawyer	_____

Local Celebrity _____

Media Personality _____

Real Estate Broker _____

Religious Leader _____

Travel Agent _____

Tree Surgeon _____

Veterinarian _____

Other Knights: **Name:**

_____   _____

_____   _____

_____   _____

_____   _____

_____   _____

_____   _____

Need more? Don't stop here. Get more paper!

Many years ago, I visited Africa and there was a hotel where you sat in the safety of a cocktail lounge. On the cocktail napkin was an "animal checklist." Each time you saw a giraffe or an elephant go by, you'd check it off.

At the risk of sounding cynical, make the above your mental cocktail napkin and, at all cocktail parties and other events, look for the various humans you need in your life. There are a few folks who are potentially more necessary to you than any of the above. The ones I'm talking about have the ability to help you in more important ways than the best lawyer, the highest ranking politician in your town, or the biggest celebrity. Can you guess who they are? (Hint: no, it's not your family.)

Before I tell you the answer, let me hop up on my soapbox and, while I'm preaching away, maybe you can guess the answer.

Our country is blessed with freedom— freedom to move, freedom to go into any line of work we want, freedom to have any type of friends we wish, freedom to follow any religion, and freedom to bring up our children as we please. The United States is truly a wonderful melting pot and is becoming more diverse as we speak. Our lifestyles are in a constant state of flux. The only thing constant about the United States is change.

Today, one-fourth of our population is people of color— African-American, Hispanic, Asian—and is becoming more diverse as you read this. By 2030, that will be 43 percent and will hit half by 2050.

Also our lifestyles are becoming more diverse. We are driving less and telecommuting more. Seventy-five percent of women ages 25 to 34 are now working, and 60 percent of all women are working.

It's not just diversity in the workplace. There is diversity in our neighborhoods too. In any one-mile radius it is not unusual to find representatives of all these cultures. The money is no longer primarily in the banks of Caucasians. In fact the most affluent households in the United States are Asian/Pacific Islanders who are better educated and have the highest income per household. Additionally, we have more than six million people from Mexico and one million from the Philippines living in the United States.[77]

Concerning lifestyle, it is not unusual to find office working moms and dads living next-door to stay-at-home not working moms and dads, living next-door to telecommuting moms and dads, living next-door to home business moms and dads.

Corporations are spending millions of dollars on the laudable effort to promote understanding and better communication between genders and races when it comes to working together. As communication increases, wonderful cross-cultural friendships have developed in the workplace.

Have you guessed where I'm going with this now? Right, where we need more communicating and friendship is in our neighborhoods. It is rare today for people to know more than twenty of their neighbors. (In New York City where I live, it's unusual if anyone knows *anyone* who lives nearby—including their next-door neighbors!)

Several years ago I was on a business trip when an embarrassingly complimentary article about my speaking engagements came out in a magazine. They had even published my phone number so, naturally, I fantasized my phone ringing off the hook with dozens of big deal prospective clients calling me.

The day after it was on the newsstands, I couldn't wait to beep in for messages. I had my pen and pad all poised to write down their numbers. My phone rang once, twice, and then a curt computer-generated voice from my answering machine informed its owner saying, "Sorry, this machine is not taking messages. Good-bye."

Good-bye! Thanks a lot. That's what all my big-deal prospective clients were going to hear, and that's what it was going to be all right, good-bye clients.

I figured out what happened. When rerecording, I must have hit the wrong button and left it on the computer-generated outgoing only message setting. My machine wasn't exactly state of the art, and there was no way I could correct the problem by remote. But with a simple push of a button by a live human being, my machine could have been instantly purring away again with my brilliant outgoing message designed to dazzle prospective clients.

But who was I going to call? My roommate was away and no one else in the building had the key. And even if they had, I wouldn't have felt comfortable asking them that favor. That is a sad commentary of the lonely life in a big city.

I have since told this story in my seminars and was surprised that many participants who live in smaller communities in much more civil parts of the country would have had the same problem. When there's a problem—"who ya gonna call?"

63 "Who Ya Gonna Call?"

Think about it. Suppose you are at a business dinner at a restaurant an hour away from home. The maître d' comes to your table to tell you have an urgent phone call. You discover it's your babysitter and she sounds hysterical. She tells you your three-year-old has locked herself in the bathroom and is crying uncontrollably. *Who ya gonna call?*

Now, let's say you're sound asleep one night. You get a panicked call from your brother-in-law. He thinks your pregnant sister is about to go into labor, and his car won't start.

"Stay calm," you tell him, "I'll be right over." As you jump into your jeans, you remember, "Oh no, *my* car's in the shop being fixed!" *Who ya gonna call?*

Or what about this one—has it ever happened to you? It has me. You're happily driving in your car on the thruway humming to the music. Then the AP news comes on. Usual stuff—waging war and rioting in faraway places. Disastrous hurricanes, tornadoes, or downpours in faraway places. Political news from faraway D.C. Then comes the local news. Top story—a fire raging in *Ohmygod that's* my *neighborhood*! Your foot presses the accelerator almost to the floor. You risk getting a ticket but you need to know whether your house is still a house or a charred pulp. You zap into the next rest stop and race to the phone bank, but . . . *Who ya gonna call?*

Dozens of problems arise throughout the year where calling a good neighbor is the solution.

64 Making Deposits in the Good Neighbor Account

Just like you need to put money into a bank account before you can draw any out, you need to put some emotional investment into your neighbors before you can draw any favors out.

How do you put value in the Good Neighbor account? In a myriad of ways. Take the time to stop and chat when you meet on the street. Give a small party and invite the neighbors. Those who don't know everyone in the neighborhood will be especially grateful. It gives them the opportunity to meet the other neighbors when they might be too shy to take the initiative on their own.

Invite some neighbors to dinner or brunch. If there are television show *events* you know you are both going to watch, invite them over to see it with you. If you know they like a particular actor or director and you have the video, invite them to come view it with you. Folks living alone will really value this. People with families often don't realize as the shadows start to fall the loneliness of the long evening ahead for many who live alone.

Remember your neighbors when you're traveling and buy them a small present. Or better yet, buy their kids a tiny gift. You can also send them a card remembering their "Special Day."

Do you live in a neighborhood where most of the folks are married, and there are only one or two single or divorced people? You meet someone you think they'd hit it off with? Give them a *surprise*. Fix the two of them up on a blind date. Now that's a great present!

Call after a big snowstorm or other weather-related headline to see if your neighbors suffered any damage. That's treating them like *family* and letting them know you are there for them. It's wonderful, especially for older folks, to know one of their neighbors cares.

If new people move into your neighborhood, invite them to tea. (Hey, this is nothing new. In 1922, Emily Post practically laid down the law. You *must* invite new neighbors over for tea.)

Someday your neighbors may be the most important *family* members you have, and all due to proximity.

♀♂

CLAUSE #54:

GOOD NEIGHBOR CLAUSE

I will make one of the following deposits in my Good Neighbor Account, a minimum of once a month.

1. Give a party.
2. Call a new neighbor.
3. Invite a neighbor to dinner or weekend brunch.
4. Invite a neighbor to "watch the game," "watch the Academy Awards," etc.
5. Give a little gift to them or their kids.
6. Plan a nice surprise—a blind date for singles?
7. Make two friendly phone calls, especially to lonely neighbors.

_____

65 Give Yourself a Priceless Gift

"Maybe it all began at Camp Mohawk. Hmm, or was it that double date in my dad's old Ford? No, No, it must have been when we sat next to each other in, ugh, Latin. Whenever it started, we swore we'd be friends for life. Where is she now?" I wonder.

"He was the first boy who ever slipped his hand under my sweater and whispered 'I love you' in my ear. The stars were like fireworks when we both looked up at their flickering and promised to be together forever. Where is he now?" I wonder.

For some strange reason memories like these flash on my windshield whenever I'm driving in a new city. Maybe it's because I don't know where they live now and every once in a while someone passes me on the highway who looks like a long lost friend or love. I floor the gas pedal.

But then, I have to remind myself that whoever passed looked like my friends did *then*, not now.

It is said if you stand on the corner of 42nd Street and Broadway in New York City, sooner or later you'll see everyone you ever knew. I spend a lot of time on that corner in the half-price theater tickets line. Sometimes I mutter to myself "old hippie" when a long-haired beggar asks for a handout. Or I whisper to a girl-friend how a passing mink-clad socialite has an obvious face-lift.

Could that old hippie be the boy who gave me my first kiss under the stars? Could the obviously pruned matron be the pal I swore eternal friendship with? So many people I once called "my best friend" have passed me by or pulled off on the shoulder and disappeared in my rearview mirror. People I once trusted with my deepest darkest secrets are now strangers to me.

A little over a year ago, I was surfing the Web after an especially pensive drive from Los Angeles down the coastal highway to San Diego in a blinding rainstorm. As though my fingers were on a Ouija board, I started typing in the names of old friends whose faces had flashed before me with each swipe of the windshield wipers. A dozen or so came up with no matches, but I had three good hits.

I found Irene, my best friend in college. She wanted to be a fado singer. Her name came up as a fund-raiser who brought musical troupes from Lisbon to America. And there was Ricky, my first boyfriend, with his very own Web page. Ricky was going to raise polo horses professionally. His page didn't mention polo horses, but it did tell about his Ford dealership in our hometown. And Jayne, a real Anglophile. She was going to be Ambassador to England. Her name came on screen in a list of people who had spoken at The English Speaking Union.

What if their fingers had clicked on my page? Would they all smile, remembering my exaggerated dreams, only to find the reality so different too?

I debated long and hard before calling them. Each lived in a different city so I decided to leave it to destiny. If my work ever took me to within several hundred miles of them, it would be fate's hand pushing us together.

I have seen all three now and wouldn't trade the experience for a thousand dollars. Ricky and I remembered the days when our mere touch was a wonder, and our whispers sounded like thunder. Jayne and I laughed until we cried. Irene and I even rolled on the floor in hysterics. The intensity of emotion was something we all forgot we were even capable of.

Would I want to see them again? Would they want to see me again? Probably not. But the one meeting with each was so special, that I beseech you to do the same. Whatever new friends or lovers you find through using the clauses in *How to Be a People Magnet*, please enrich your life with the old ones as well.

♀♂

CLAUSE #55:

FIND AN OLD FRIEND OR OLD LOVE

I will look up at least one old friend and (if I'm not hurting my current love) one old love. I will spend a few hours with them—no expectations other than maybe savoring the special sentiments we once shared. (And probably realizing why I left him or her in my rearview mirror.) Whatever happens, or doesn't, I know we will both receive a priceless gift. We will each come away with a fresh and profound new sense of self.

 _____

♡ Endnotes

1. Potts, Marilyn K. "Social Support and Depression Among Older Adults Living Alone: The Importance of Friends Within and Outside of a Retirement Community." *Social Work* 42 (1997): 340–363.

2. Rotundo, E. A. *American Manhood: Transformations in Masculinity from the Revolution to the Modern Era.* New York: Basic Books, 1993.

3. Snyder, M., E. Berscheid, and P. Glick. "Focusing Relationships." *Journal of Personality and Social Psychology* 48 (1985): 1427–1439.

4. Aleman, Anna M. Martiez. "Understanding and Investigating Female Friendship's Educative Value." *Journal of Higher Education* 68 (1997): 119–140.

5. Sternberg, R. J., and S. Grajek. "The Nature of Love." *Journal of Personality and Social Psychology* 47 (1998): 12–29.

6. Wright, Paul H. "Men's Friendships, Women's Friendships, and the Alleged Inferiority of the Latter." *Sex Roles: A Journal of Research* 8 (1982): 1–20.

7. Roberto, Karen A. "Qualities of Older Women's Friendships: Stable or Volatile." *International Journal of Aging and Human Development* 44 (1997): 1–15.

8. Wartik, Nancy. "The Surprising Link to Longer Life." *McCall's* 124 (1997): 104–109.

9. Mallow, T. E., A. Yarlas, R. K. Montvilo, and D. B. Sugarman. "Agreement and Accuracy in Children's Interpersonal Perceptions: A Social Relations Analysis." *Journal of Personality and Social Psychology* 67 (1995): 692–702.

10. O'Brien, S. F., and K. L. Bierman. "Conceptions of Perceived Influence of Peer Groups: Interviews with Pre-adolescent and Adolescents." *Child Development* 59 (1998): 1360–1365.

11. Merten, D. E. "The Meaning of Meanness: Popularity, Competition, and Conflict Among Junior High School Girls." *Sociology of Education* 70 (1997): 175–191.

12. Sprecher, Susan. "Insiders' Perspectives on Reasons for Attractions to a Close Other." *Social Psychology Quarterly* 61 (1998): 287.

13. Burgoon, J. K. "Interpersonal Expectations, Expectancy Violations, and Emotional Communication." *Social Psychology Quarterly* 61 (1993): 287.

14. LaFontana, Kathryn M., and Antonius H. N. Cillessen. "Children's Interpersonal Perceptions as a Function of Sociometric and Peer-Perceived Popularity." *Journal of Genetic Psychology* 160 (1999): 225.

15. "The Possible Woman." Annual women's leadership conference organized by Linda Wind of Kennesaw State University: possiblewoman@mindspring.com.

16. James, Deborah, and Sandra Clarke. "Women, Men and Interruptions: A Critical Review." In *Gender and Conversational Interaction*, edited by Deborah Tannen, 231–280. New York: Oxford University Press, 1993.

17. Clancy, Patricia. "The Acquisition of Communicative Style in Japanese." In *Language Acquisition and Socialization Across Cultures*, edited by Bambi B. Schieffelin and Elinor Ochs, 213–250. Cambridge: Cambridge University Press, 1986.

18. Ueda, Kieko. "Sixteen Ways to Avoid Saying 'No' in Japan." In *Intercultural Encounters with Japan: Communication—Contact and Conflict*, edited by J. C. Condon and M. Saito, 184–192. Tokyo: Simul., 1974.

19. Sobal, J., and A. J. Stunkard. "Socioeconomic Status and Obesity: A Review of the Literature." *Psychological Bulletin* 105 (1989): 260–275.

20. Anderson, J. L., C. B. Crawford, J. Nadeau, and T. Lidnberg. "Was the Duchess of Windsor Right: A Cross-Cultural Review of the Socioecology of Ideals of Female Body Shape." *Ethology and Sociobiology* 13 (1992): 197–227.

21. Harrison, Kristen. "Does Interpersonal Attraction to Thin Media Personalities Promote Eating Disorders?" *Journal of Broadcasting & Electronic Media* 41 (1997): 478–501.

22. Smith, Jane E., et al. "Single White Male Looking for Thin, Very Attractive . . ." *Sex Roles* 23 (1990): 675–685.

23. Barber, Nigel. "Secular Changes in Standards of Bodily Attractiveness in American Women: Different Masculine and Feminine Ideals." *Journal of Psychology* 132 (1998): 87–95.

24. Wiederman, Michael W., and Shannon R. Hurst. "Body Size, Physical Attractiveness, and Body Image Among Young Adult Women: Relationships to Sexual Experience and Sexual Esteem." *Journal of Sex Research* 35 (1998): 272–282.

25. Czechowicz, H., and C. L. Diaz de Chumaceiro. "Psychosomatics of Beauty and Ugliness: Theoretical

Implications of the Systems Approach." *Clinical Dermatol (CLD)* 6 (1997): 9–14.

26. The National Speakers Association annual conference, July 1997, opening address by several of the officers.

27. Morman, Mark T., and Kory Floyd. "Overt Expression of Affection in Male-Male Interaction." *Journal of Research* 38 (1998): 871–882.

28. Arkowitz, H., et al. "The Behavioral Assessment of Social Competence in Males." *Behavioral Therapy* 6 (1975): 3–13.

29. Henderson, Lynn. "Mean MMPI Profile of Referrals to a Shyness Clinic." *Psychological Reports* 80 (1997): 695–703.

30. Pilkonis, P. A., C. Heape, and R. H. Klein. "Treating Shyness and Other Psychiatric Difficulties in Psychiatric Outpatients." *Communication Education* 29 (1980): 250–255.

31. Izard, C. E., and M. C. Hyson. "Shyness as a Discrete Emotion." In *Shyness: Perspectives on Research and Treatment*, edited by W. H. Jones, J. M. Cheek, and S. R. Briggs, 147–160. New York: Plenum, 1986.

32. Hamer, R. J., and M. A. Bruch. "Personality Factors and Inhibited Career Development: Testing the Unique Contribution of Shyness." *Journal of Vocational Behavior* 50 (1997): 382–400.

33. Sanderson, W. C., P. A. DiNardo, R. M. Rapee, and D. H. Barlow. "Syndrome Co-Morbidity in Patients Diagnosed with DSM-III Revised Anxiety Disorder." *Journal of Abnormal Psychology* 99 (1990): 308–312.

34. Capsi, A., G. H. Elder, and D. J. Bern. "Moving Away from the World: Life-Course Patterns of Shy Children." *Developmental Psychology* 24 (1988): 824–831.

35. Garcia, S., L. Stinson, W. Ickes, V. Bissonnette, and S. Briggs. "Shyness and Physical Attractiveness in

Mixed-Sex Dyads." *Journal of Personality and Social Psychology* 61 (1991) 35–49.

36. Bruch, M. A., J. Gorsky, T. M. Collins, and P. A. Berger. "Shyness and Sociability Re-examined: A Multicomponent Analysis." *Journal of Personality and Social Psychology* 57 (1989): 904–915.

37. Cheek, J. M., and A. H. Buss. "Shyness and Sociability." *Journal of Personality and Social Psychology* 41 (1981): 330–339.

38. Goode, Erica. "Social Anxiety, Old as Society Itself," *New York Times,* 20 October 1998.

39. Noriyuki, Duane. "Breaking Down the Walls," *Los Angeles Times,* 5 February 1996.

40. Lowndes, Leil. *How to Make Anyone Fall in Love with You.* Lincolnwood: NTC/Contemporary Publishing, 1996.

41. Walster, Elaine, William G. Walster, and Ellen Berscheid. *Equity: Theory and Research.* Boston: Allyn and Bacon, 1978.

42. Morman, Mark T., and Kory Floyd. "Overt Expression of Affection in Male-Male Interaction." *Journal of Research* 38 (1998) 871–882.

43. Rabinowitz, F. E. "The Male-to-Male Embrace: Breaking the Touch Taboo in a Men's Therapy Group." *Journal of Counseling and Development* 69 (1991): 574–576.

44. Shotland, R., et al. "Can Men and Women Differentiate Between Friendly and Sexually Interested Behavior?" *Social Psychology Quarterly* 51 (1988): 66–73.

45. LaFontana, Kathryn M., and Antonius H. N. Cillessen. "Children's Interpersonal Perceptions as a Function of Sociometric and Peer-Perceived Popularity." *Journal of Genetic Psychology* 160 (1999): 225.

46. Adler., P. A., S. J. Kless, and P. Adler. "Socialization to Gender Roles: Popularity Among Elementary School Boys and Girls." *Sociology of Education* 65 (1992): 169–187.

47. *New York Times*, 24 April 1999, p. 14.

48. Garcia, S., L. Stinson., W. Ickes., V. Bissonnette, and S. Briggs. "Shyness and Physical Attractiveness in Mixed-Sex Dyads." *Journal of Personality and Social Psychology* 61 (1991): 35–49.

49. Kowner, Rotem. "The Effect of Physical Attractiveness Comparison on Choice of Partners." *Journal of Social Psychology* 4 (1995): 153.

50. Mitchell, W. *It's Not What Happens to You, It's What You Do About It*. Smyrna, GA: Phoenix Press, 1997.

51. One of W. Mitchell's inspirational speeches.

52. Liebowitz, M. R. *The Chemistry of Love*. Boston: Little Brown, 1983.

53. Mead, Margaret. *Sex and Temperament in Three Primitive Societies*. New York: William Morrow, 1935.

54. Liebowitz, M. R. *The Chemistry of Love*. Boston: Little Brown, 1983.

55. Ibid.

56. Murray, Sandra L., and John G. Holmes. "Seeing Virtues in Faults: Negativity and the Transformation of Interpersonal Narratives in Close Relationships." *Journal of Personality and Social Psychology* (65): 707–723.

57. Fisher, Helen. "The Four-Year Itch." *Natural History* (1989): 22–23.

58. Ibid.

59. Liebowitz, M. R. *The Chemistry of Love*. Boston: Little Brown, 1983.

60. Gagnon, Robert Michael, and Stuart Michaels. *The Social Organization of Sexuality*. Chicago: University of Chicago Press, 1994.

61. Byrne, Donn. *The Attraction Paradigm*. New York: Academic Press, 1971.

62. Dutton, D. G., and A. P. Aron. "Some Evidence for Heightened Sexual Attraction Under Conditions of High Anxiety." *Journal of Personality and Social Psychology* 30 (1974): 510–517.

63. Byrne, Donn. *The Attraction Paradigm*. New York: Academic Press, 1971.

64. Ibid.

65. Perper, Timothy. *Sex Signals: The Biology of Love*. Philadelphia: ISI Press, 1985.

66. Oguchi, Takashi, et al. "Voice and Interpersonal Attraction." *Japanese Psychological Research* 39 (1997): 56–61.

67. Shumaker, S. A., and D. R. Hill. "Gender Differences in Social Support and Physical Health." *Health Psychology* 10 (1991): 102–111.

68. Moller, Lora C., et al. "Sex Typing in Play and Popularity in Middle Childhood." *Sex Roles: A Journal of Research* 26 (1992): 331.

69. Barbee, Anita P., et al. "Effects of Gender Role Expectations on the Social Support Process." *Journal of Social Issues* 49 (1993): 175–191.

70. Ibid.

71. Carli, L. L. "Gender Differences in Interaction Style and Influence: Correction." *Journal of Personality and Social Psychology* 57 (1989): 964.

72. Moller, Lora C., et al. "Sex Typing in Play and Popularity in Middle Childhood." *Sex Roles: A Journal of Research* 26 (1992): 331.

73. James, Deborah, and Janice Drakich. "Understanding Gender Differences in Amount of Talk." MS, Linguistics Department, University of Toronto.

74. Ibid.

75. Ibid.

76. Lakoff, Robin. *Language and Woman's Places*. New York: Harper and Row, 1975.

77. Dupont, Kay. *Handling Diversity in the Workplace*. Monteray, CA: American Media Publishing, 1997.

Have you found more great ways to be a People Magnet? If so, send me an E-mail so I can share the hint with other readers. (And let me know if I can credit you!) Maybe you would just like to be added to my E-dress book and receive additional "Magnetic Power Attraction" hints from time to time. Or find out when People Magnet seminars are coming to your area. E-mail me at leil@peoplemagnet.com. Hope to hear from you!

About the Author

Leil Lowndes is a dynamic speaker and internationally recognized communications expert who presents programs in practically every major U.S. city. She coaches Fortune 500 executives on interpersonal communications and conducts seminars for the U.S. Peace Corps, foreign governments, and major corporations. She is the author of four books, including the top-selling *How to Talk to Anybody About Anything, How to Make Anyone Fall in Love with You*, and *Talking the Winner's Way*. Leil has appeared on hundreds of television and radio shows. For further information on the author, visit www.lowndes.com.